LIQUEURS

TO MY PARENTS

Liqueurs

Peter Hallgarten
Ph.D. (London), F.R.I.C.

Wine & Spirit Publications Ltd.

By the same Author

Châteauneuf-du-Pape 1961
Côtes-du-Rhône (2nd Edition) 1972
Wineograph (6th Edition) 1973
Liqueurograph (3rd Edition) 1973

1

Printed in Great Britain
for Wine & Spirit Publications Ltd.,
Southbank House, Black Prince Road, London, S.E.1
by S. Straker & Sons Ltd., London

CONTENTS

v

FOREWORD

My association with liqueurs was neither premeditated nor expected; I was asked suddenly to take over a Glen Mist compounding operation in 1961. From that memorable day, when I made a very worried and nervous start, I have become fascinated by the world of liqueurs, the history of their development, their popularity in past centuries and the introduction of modern post-war liqueurs; all of this led to deep involvement, experimentation and development of my own new liqueurs.

The absence of a modern book on liqueurs was an obvious gap which required filling and in this short treatise, I have attempted to cover ground which is both of interest to the Wine and Spirit Trade as well as the consumer, be he a novice or connoisseur.

I would like to record my thanks to the numerous liqueur houses and their importers who provided background material about many of the liqueurs, and to my Maurice Meyer co-directors, who allowed me free use of the company's copyright material. My special thanks are due to my father, Pat Simon and Gerard McCarten, who assisted me with encouragement and criticism, to Robert Gross and Dr. Kleipol for special information, and to my wife for writing the chapter on 'Liqueurs in the kitchen,' and encouraging the writing of this book.

LONDON 1967.

vii

SPECIAL NOTE

The alcoholic strengths quoted in the text are British proof unless otherwise stated. For conversion to Continental and American units see Chapter 7.

Chapter 1

LIQUEURS

LIQUEURS, which are known as cordials in the U.S.A., are basically nothing more than sweetened and flavoured alcoholic beverages. They are frequently referred to as digestives, particularly in France, where the *Digestif* is enjoyed after a meal, and was so named because of the large number of herbs, etc., with soothing properties which are to be found in the older established liqueurs.

The term has also been applied to old brandies and old malt whiskies which have been matured in cask for many years, and which have obtained the flavour, qualities and smoothness of a compounded liqueur, without the sweetness.

In New York, where half bottles of whisky cannot by law be sold, whisky is available in slightly sweetened form in half-bottle size, when it is called Scotch Whisky Liqueur.

Liqueurs can be colourless or highly coloured, with various degrees of sweetness, and of high or low alcoholic strength. Preference is very personal, and must always be considered as a combination of sense reactions. The gold flakes in *goldwasser;* the brilliant red of *cherry brandy*; the mellow gold of *Glen Mist;* the icy green of *Royal Mint*—all attract the eye and stimulate the palate, as does the bouquet of many fruit liqueurs and *eaux-de-vie*.

In the fifth century B.C. Hippocrates is said to have practised the art of distillation and the blending of herbs and aromatic plants, but the product may have been a crude vermouth based on wine and not on spirit. It is said of early blenders that such concoctions based on aromatised wine were very potent and inebriating, and therefore fit only for the strongest of men! Five hundred years later, Pliny, the famous Roman naturalist, reported such distillation and spoke of a Faustino wine which burnt *De Faustino vino flamma accendi* and there is no doubt that the Ancients skilfully extracted liquid perfume from aromatic plants. Bas-reliefs representing alembics (distillation vessels) were even found in the Temple of Memphis.

It is, of course, obvious that liqueurs have both digestive and curative properties, and when we read of Herbal wines of the middle ages, these beverages were produced by steeping herbs in grape juice, and amongst others, absinthe, aloes, aniseed, hyssop, myrtle, centaury, rosemary, sage and many more were used. Enthusiastic descriptions are frequently found in the literature of the time, and of course, these herbal wines were indispensable as prescriptions by doctors for the sick. The best were known as *vins herbés* and contained honey and Asian spices.

Liqueurs as we know them, however, are thought to have been invented by monks, who, frequently acting as medical men, were interested in herbs and plants, and by appreciating the products of mother nature, discovered the beauty and benefits of liqueurs.

Dioscorides, a celebrated Sicilian doctor and contemporary of Tiberius, indicated the first primitive distillation apparatus; there is no doubt that the Arabs had a knowledge of these processes. Avicennus, an Arab philosopher-doctor of A.D. 980 in fact discussed two alcoholic products in his writings, and Rhazes, the famous Doctor of Carthage, is said to have described, exactly, three distillations! The Chinese are recorded as producing ' alaki ' (araki) from rice wines in the thirteenth century, but are thought to have done so as early as 800 B.C.

As time went by, the products were improved and with each generation, as the secrets were handed down, slight variations were bound to occur. Communication was by word of mouth and formulae were hardly ever written down. Nowadays, of course, formulae can have great commercial value, and with the ever-present risks of modern life, most holders of liqueur secrets make use of bank vaults to ensure continuity of their famous products.

French researchers believe that Arnaud de Villeneuve and Lulle in the thirteenth century rediscovered *eaux-de-vie* distillation; the former wrote that the distillate should be kept in golden vessels not to impair its quality. He recorded that *eaux-de-vie*, in which rosemary and sage had been steeped, were soothing to the nerves!

They produced the first recorded French liqueur, *l'eau clairette*, a sweetened *eau-de-vie*, scented with lemon, rose leaves and other aromatic herbs. The product was decorated with specks of gold in the belief that ' nature had endowed gold with the most admirable virtues.'

German literature seems quite clear that distillation was invented between 1050 and 1150. The work of Magister Salernus is quoted, who made ' *aqua ardens* ' in the twelfth century.

In the fifteenth century, Michel Savonarole is credited with distillation from a metal container and subsequent cooling of the hot vapours in a cold water bath. He described, in his book ' De Aqua Vitae,' the work of the Franciscan monk de Rupescissa, with wine, roots, fruits and herbs.

By the middle ages, Italy had also become a liqueur producer, with centres of production in Florence, Venice and Turin. Catherine de Medici is supposed to have enjoyed them and to have made them popular in France, and a liqueur recipe of that time consisting of brandy, water, sugar musk, amber, aniseed and cinnamon is reported to have rejuvenated the ageing Louis XIV. These liqueurs include ' *le rossoli*,' which were liqueurs of many recipes, and ' *le populo*,' which was sweetened wine spirit flavoured with natural products.

In 1638, in the reign of King Charles I, the Worshipful Company of Distillers was incorporated in London, the charter of which conferred upon the Company the extensive powers and important duties in the regulation of the Trade of Distillers and Vinegar makers, and of those engaged in the preparation of artificial and strong waters in the Cities of London and Westminster.

After the Revolution the French distillers established themselves with rules for apprenticeships, admission as a ' *chef d'oeuvre* ' and dispensation for sons of ' masters.' Widows were permitted to work but not to be apprenticed. In 1747, French distillers came within the jurisdiction of the local courts for the control of the preparation of drugs and herbal remedies.

Seventeenth century literature has frequent references to *ratafias* and similar products being served, and there are several German treatises on the manufacture of wines and their distillation.

Recorded liqueurs from the eighteenth century include *aquavit* flavoured with angelica, cardamom, citrus fruits, coffee and various herbal flavours. *Persiko* was a peach leaf distillate, and aniseed, rose and celery ratafias were produced. The finished liqueurs were coloured with natural products and even filtered before sale.

The nineteenth century saw great progress made in distillation and acceptance of new techniques. Areas became famous for special products: Amsterdam (*curaçao*), Bordeaux (*anisette*), Marseilles (*absinthe*), Grenoble (*ratafias*), Dijon (*cassis*), Paris (*all liqueurs*) and, of course, many monasteries all over France produced their own specialities. Some of these liqueurs used more than 100 different ingredients to produce the final product. It is interesting that the magnificent French green and yellow herb liqueurs, which were originated in monasteries, have not been equalled by any other liqueur producing country—most of which are Protestant!

The first French liqueur was probably *l'eau clairette*, of Villeneuve, already described, and then came the liqueurs of Montpelier, of Lorraine (*parfait amour*) and, of course, the ratafias, cherry and blackcurrant, which still retain their popularity.

Local distilleries were started in mountain regions, where the compounding and distillation were facilitated by herbs, spices and fruits being readily available within immediate reach.

Although France and Holland are the best known, all fruit-growing countries produce their own liqueurs and frequently *eaux-de-vie* as well. In many cases the latter are ' whiskies ' from cereals.

5

Emphasis in this short treatise has obviously been placed on liqueurs which are well known, mainly in the U.K. and the U.S.A., many of which have become brand leaders to the exclusion of similar products, which, through commercial considerations, have not received the support of advertising.

There are many very fine liqueurs produced in Germany, Italy, the Iron Curtain countries, Spain, Australia, Japan, etc., which are not imported because they would not be commercially viable propositions in competition with equivalent products which have been known for decades. A few Israeli liqueurs are exported, which are manufactured in accordance with dietary laws of food preparation and thus Kosher. They can therefore be enjoyed by religious Jews. I recall the superb Australian liqueurs which were imported after the war, which were thoroughly enjoyed until the Dutch and French liqueurs returned, when the old European names rapidly replaced the new liqueurs. The British liqueur industry is thriving, although on a more rational basis then before the war. Many products are no longer being manufactured, but the best play an important role in the export drive.

One of the most interesting developments of the past decade is the manufacture, under licence, of Dutch and French liqueurs in the U.S.A. and recently Dutch liqueurs in Australia, using local spirit but the original flavour concentrate which is shipped in bulk. Some famous gins are rectified in New Jersey, and in certain countries Scotch malt whisky is blended with local grain spirit, producing a ' Scotch type whisky ' which can be very palatable—the line, however, must be drawn when these whiskies are represented as pure Scotch whisky. The Scotch Whisky Association is most vigilant and takes action against fraudulent representation of true Scotch whisky.

The secret of a good liqueur is its flavour, its perfume, the fine balance of the alcohol (which must be present but not obvious) and the cohesive sweetness—essentially a smooth homogeneous liquid, of enticing and entrancing perfume and colour. The word liqueur is derived from the Latin *lique-facere*, to melt, make liquid or dissolve, and is a solution in which the essential elements must be intricately and irreversibly mixed and dissolved.

Thousands of liqueurs are known, produced in many countries in most parts of the world, and it would be impossible to name them all in this book. Those that are known to me are discussed in a later section. Turning back the pages of history it is amusing to note some of the many liqueurs invented to celebrate a special occasion or designed to appear as elixirs or medicines or solely to titillate the imagination: *Venus Oil, Cream of the Virgin, Harems' Delight, The good minded Empress, Parfait amour*, and many others.

Chapter 2

THE DEVELOPMENT OF LIQUEURS

THE production of liqueurs in past centuries was naturally in the hands of monks in the abbeys and monasteries of Europe. The medical benefits were apparent side by side with the purely sensual pleasure of drinking them and these early rough and ready mixtures frequently helped save life during the plague and disease ridden years of our history. No doubt they were also used then as we use them now, as an enjoyable relaxant and restorative at the end of the meal. That such mixtures would have tonic powers seems obvious from the ingredients used, and although the early liqueurs were in all probability harsh to the taste, and more like medicine of today, with time they were improved, maybe by ageing in wooden casks or by altering the ingredients or by changing the method of production.

The logical extension was to produce liqueurs for enjoyment only with the medicinal benefits becoming of secondary importance. The most famous instance was the invention of a liqueur by the French doctor, Raspail, whose cure was enjoyed so much that it became commercial and world renowned. The *goldwasser* produced today is a combination of two medical superstitions, that gold was a perfect foil for diseases and caraway was the best digestive, the latter used even now for winding babies after feeds (but called gripe water and only 4½ per cent. alcohol.) Many restaurants on the Continent and America provide peppermints for diners, which is supposedly good for digestion and recommend *crème de menthe* as *digestif.* Very popular in Britain now are the after-dinner chocolate-mints, and the liqueur of comparable flavour ' *Royal Mint-Chocolate.*'

The historical background of the various liqueurs will be examined in a later section.

Chapter 3

THE ART OF TASTING

IT is said that the art of tasting must be inborn, and that it is impossible to become an expert without this inherited quality. There is no doubt that there is a certain truth in this statement that those born into a family experienced in the art of tasting have great benefit, especially of environment, which from an early age teaches the evaluation of sensual messages to the eye, the nose and the mouth. The art of tasting, however, can be learnt but it requires hard work and continuous application. It is obviously easier to study sweet liqueurs with well defined flavours than wines with their subtleties; in the latter, the lower alcoholic strength defines small differences more strongly, which are sometimes undetectable to the novice. The art of tasting must be practised endlessly and there are always fresh samples to examine or new products to consider. Naturally, anyone interested in serious tasting must have a sensitive palate which, with training, can become highly developed and expert.

The tasting of liqueurs can be, and usually is, a tiring and difficult job. Steady inhalation of liqueur bouquet will slowly anaesthetise the sensitive nasal buds and dull the senses. Tasting of several samples will desensitise the taste buds in the mouth and on the tongue, and generally mask minimal defects very seriously. I have found in my various experimental liqueur compoundings that a dozen closely similar samples is the maximum I can compare without my judgement being impaired. There is no doubt that for best results, six liqueur samples are maximum, and twelve samples may give reasonable results which, however, require further examination and confirmation after the palate has been cleansed with water and rested for an hour.

Samples should be tasted in brandy balloons if possible, which allow the bouquet to be examined and possibly give a hint of the spirit used. Bouquet is especially important in blended products which may use two types of spirit where harmonious co-existence is essential. The bouquet can give a taster many clues, but it is the combination of nose and palate which is so essential for a balanced judgement. For the palate, a small sample should be taken which can be rolled over the tongue and the sample then rejected, if possible *in toto*. The taster should consider not only the flavour and sweetness of the liqueur, but also the ' hotness ' of the spirit. The ' hotter ' or sharper the spirit, the younger it is—spirits mellow with age and older spirit is much preferable to young. Essential to all good compounding is ageing in wood, which mellows and harmonises the alcoholic and flavour ingredients, except of course for fruit spirits which are usually aged in glass demi-johns to avoid taking up colour.

The next sample should not be taken until the mouth has been rinsed with cool, clean water. In my opinion, if the taster wishes to eat between samples he should take white rolls and for liqueurs never even consider nibbling cheese. Although I am not a smoker, which may or may not increase my palate sensitivity, a smoker can often revive a flagging palate by a few puffs at a cigarette, but only out of doors in the fresh air. This certainly works when wines are under consideration and by extension, should do so for liqueurs.

Chapter 4

HOW TO DRINK AND ENJOY LIQUEURS

BASICALLY, the only important rule is that a clean glass should be used. Nothing else really matters, although enjoyment can be immensely enhanced by serving liqueurs in very thin glasses or finely cut glasses. The excitement for the taste buds seems to increase in direct ratio to the decreasing thickness of the glass!

Enjoyment of a liqueur follows a certain pattern:

(a) The beauty of the empty glass combined with the shape of the decanter or original bottle. This anticipates the liqueur itself and visually prepares the recipient for the enjoyment to follow.

(b) The colour of the liqueur and its flow from the bottle. At this stage, the physical response may stimulate the taste buds and give the mouth-watering effect.

(c) The nosing of the liqueur, the bouquet stimulating the nasal buds.

(d) The sipping of the liqueur, savouring the flavour on the palate.

(e) The climax on swallowing the liqueur, the warm glow in the stomach and the enjoyment of the after taste on the palate.

Liqueurs can be enjoyed at all times of the day, with morning coffee (*eaux-de-vie* are delicious), in a cocktail for an aperitif, with coffee after lunch; aperitif cocktail before dinner, with coffee after dinner and a liqueur to sip leisurely throughout the evening, or even as a night-time stimulant as enjoyed by Boswell with his bedside bottles of strong cordials.

In the final analysis a large glass is recommended so that the bouquet, colour and flow can be enjoyed as well as the taste, but of course, you lose more liqueur by viscous adhesion to the sides than with a small glass, as you drink.

Frequently the flavour of a liqueur will be enhanced by serving it chilled or served ' on the rocks,' which effectively reduces both the sweetness and alcohol, yet increases the beauty of the aroma, often illuminating high tone bouquet nuances which are not at all apparent when the liqueur is served at room temperature.

As with all drinking, you will obtain the maximum pleasure by drinking ' what you like, with whatever you like and when you like.'

Chapter 5

THE SPIRIT OF LIQUEURS

THE essential ingredient, common to all liqueurs, is alcohol. This may be obtained from numerous sources in a number of ways. Important to all of these is the purity; the purer the alcohol, the finer the liqueur, as by-products of alcohol production such as fusel oils, are unwanted flavour additives. As they would not necessarily be present in identical amounts in successive productions, which would yield differently flavoured end-products, skilful compounding and manipulation would be required for corrective treatment.

Spirits used in liqueurs may be of any of the following types:

1. Neutral spirit.
2. Neutral grain spirit.
3. Whisky or whiskey.
4. Rum.
5. Grape brandy or cognac or armagnac.
6. Fruit spirit.
7. Rice spirit.

The quality of the spirit will depend on the following factors:

(a) The origin and the nature of the starting materials (and the fermented liquid made from them).

(*b*) The manner of distillation (speed, temperature, pressure).

(*c*) The degree of rectification.

(*d*) The method of maturing and alcoholic strength after distillation.

Each of the types of spirits has its special uses and often blends are made between types, e.g. whisky may be a blend of grain spirit and ' pot-still ' spirit. Unless the liqueur label specifies a particular type of spirit (whisky, cognac, rum), the use of neutral or grain spirit is implied.

Chapter 6

CLASSIFICATION OF LIQUEURS

FRENCH liqueur manufacturers traditionally classify their products into four main groups, all of which are produced by distillation or infusion. The use of essential oils is infrequent and rather frowned upon. 'Ordinaires' include waters and oils. 'Fines' and 'Surfines' include Creams (*Crèmes*) and Elixirs.

LIQUEUR.—Sweetened spirit which must contain 200 gms of sugar per litre.

DEMI-FINES.—Standard strength is 40° proof (20-25 kg. sugar per 100 litres liqueur).

FINES.—Standard strength 49° proof (40-45 kg. sugar per 100 litres liqueur).

SURFINES.—The finest French liqueurs are usually 52° proof. They are the most heavily sweetened and strongest in bouquet and flavour. (45-50 kg. sugar per 100 litres liqueur.)

'*DOUBLE*' liqueurs theoretically contain double quantities of flavouring materials. More usually a 50% increase is used as many essential oils may produce cloudiness (by partial precipitation) in truly double concentration when the liqueur is diluted with water, as intended. The alcoholic strength and sweetness are identical with surfines.

TRIPLE SEC is a special term which refers to curaçaos—the word triple apparently has no definitive meaning of the manufacture, although a double rectification would give a three-stage (triple) process. *Curaçao Sec* has the sweetness of a *surfine* but a strength of 78° proof. *Triple Sec* is sweeter than *curaçao sec*, but is only 70° proof. The full range of curaçaos (demi-fine, surfine, sec, triple sec) can be made from the same basic dry high strength curaçao distillate which is then compounded with sugar and water.

RATAFIA was the name originally given to any liqueur drunk at the ratification of a treaty or agreement. Nowadays, it means liqueurs prepared by the infusion of fruits or nut kernels in spirits of wine. The liqueur is sweetened and additional flavouring may be added for completion.

CRÉME DE . . . . . is the term applied to liqueurs made only from the particular name type (vanille, menthe, roses, etc.), or is such that the named flavour is prevalent.

According to French law, the letters A and D must be printed on the label for sale in France, as follows:
Letter A (= aperitif) refers to wine-based aperitifs below 18° GL (31.5° proof), aniseed flavoured spirits below 45° GL (79° proof) (providing that they are 18° GL, less than 400 gms of sugar per litre and more than $\frac{1}{2}$ gm. essences per litre), and all bitters and similar products below 30° GL (52° proof).
Letter D (= *digestif*) refers to liqueurs and spirits above 15° GL (26.2° proof), with the exception of aniseeds and bitters, and wine-based aperitifs over 18° GL (31.5° proof).

EIS-LIKÖRE.—German liqueurs intended for drinking "on-the-rocks."

KRISTAL-LIKÖRE.—German liqueurs containing sugar crystals (c.f. Italian *Mille Fiori*).

Chapter 7

THE DECLARATION OF STRENGTH AND CONTENTS

M OST countries have laws which require the distiller, manufacturer or importer to specify the alcoholic content of his product on the label. It is unfortunate for the consumer that the chosen units vary from country to country—in the U.K. we have Proof Spirit (Sikes) which is at variance with the American unit; in many Continental countries they state alcohol by volume percentage—in some countries by weight percentage.

Normal Units:

British Proof.—Units known as Sikes.

100% alcohol = 175° proof.

Terminology:

70° proof = 30 under proof.

American Proof:

100 U.S. proof = 50% alcohol by volume

70° British proof = 80 U.S. proof.

French Alcoholic Strength is given in terms of degrees Gay-Lussac (°GL), which is the percentage alcohol by volume:

Conversion to British Units   40° GL = 70° proof.

Conversion to U.S. Units   40° GL = 80° proof.

The liquid contents of liqueurs and spirits is printed on the labels as legal requisite in many countries and most European bottle manufacturers include a figure of the total bottle capacity in the glass. This may be misleading to the consumer as this figure is the maximum liquid contents to the top lip of the bottle, and not the normal liquid content.

In Britain and the U.S.A. fluid ounces are standard, but not identical measures, whereas the metric system uses centilitres. (100 cl. = 1 litre.)

(160 fluid ozs. per British Imperial gallon.)

(128 fluid ozs. per American gallon.)

Normal Liqueur Sizes:

$26\frac{2}{3}$ Br. ozs.	$25\frac{1}{2}$ U.S. ozs. (fifth)	75 cl.
24 ,, ,,	23 ,, ,,	68 cl.
17 ,, ,,	$16\frac{1}{3}$,, ,,	50 cl.
12 ,, ,,	$11\frac{1}{2}$,, ,,	34 cl.

International discussions are in progress to establish standard bottle sizes for all countries. There is an obvious necessity for standardization, but it remains to be seen which sizes will be agreed if and when such changes become law. Until that time the combination of various alcoholic strength and liquid contents can be very confusing, and the Liqueurograph chart (pages 56/57) attempts to ease this problem and also classify liqueur types.

Chapter 8

THE RAW MATERIALS FOR FLAVOURING LIQUEURS

INNUMERABLE natural products from all parts of the world are suitable for preparing liqueurs and bitters. It is not practical to list all of these products, but those which are most frequently referred to are classified according to their natural characteristics. The methods of extraction of the actual flavouring component(s) are described in the next chapter. Many of the extracted compounds have very strong flavours, and only minute quantities are used in any compounding.

HERBS

Basil, bison and other grasses, centaury, sweet clover, coca leaves, genip, herb ivy, hyssop, knapweed, marjoram, melissa, peppermint and other mint types, polybody, rosemary, sage, tansy, tarragon, tea leaves, bitter thistle, thyme, trefoil clover, wormwood.

BARKS AND WOODS

Aloe, angostura, cinchona, cinnamon, guaiacum, myrrh, sandalwood, sassafras.

DRUGS AND ROOTS

Alant, angelica, blackmasterwort, calamus, celery, cloves,

curcuma, galanga, gentian, ginger, henna, liquorice, lovage, orris root, rhubarb, snake root, turmeric, valerian, zedoary.

FLOWERS

Arnica, camomile, cinnamon, citrus blossom, clove, ivy, lavender, lily, poplar buds, rose, saffron.

SEEDS AND FRUITS

Allspice (pimento), angelica seeds, aniseed, apricot stones, bitter almonds, cactus, cardamom, caraway (carvi and cumin), celery seeds, citrus peel, clove, cocoa, coffee, coriander, cubebs, dill (soy beans), fennel, hazel nuts, juniper berries, kola nuts, mace, musk, nutmeg, peach stones, peppers (all types), raisins, star anis, sweet almonds, tonka beans, vanilla.

This section also includes all edible fruits.

MISCELLANEOUS

Honey (various types).

Chapter 9

MANUFACTURE OF LIQUEURS

THE flavour of liqueurs and many spirits is imparted by important groups of compounds of complicated chemical structures known as essential oils, which themselves, are unpleasant and often irritating, but which in minute quantities impart ethereal and taste effects of unimaginable beauty and finesse.

Essential oils are usually liquid, but may, under certain circumstances, solidify. Each oil has its own characteristic bouquet, most are bitter to the taste and all oxidise readily and must, therefore, be stored most carefully.

These important oils can be extracted by four methods:

(*a*) Pressure: oils are extracted from citrus peel under pressure in a mechanical press.

(*b*) Extraction with a non-volatile compound. Fats, for instance, take up the bouquets, etc., and these can later be alcohol extracted.

(*c*) Extraction with a volatile solvent (maceration and percolation).

(*d*) Distillation which may be from aqueous solution, alcoholic solution or from a fractionation of a mixture of oils, or even a combination of these.

These oils, together with other flavouring substances, are extracted from the many natural compounds used in the making of liqueurs; fruits, herbs, spices, roots, flowers, berries and leaves. The extraction of flavours is followed by compounding (which may include distillation), maturing and subsequently presentation for sale.

Selection of method of manufacture depends upon many circumstances, most of which are the personal selection of the inventor or manufacturer. Whichever method is used, best results can only be obtained by use of the finest ingredients—the spirit, the sugar and/or honey, and the flavouring materials. The delicate balance between herbs, spices, flavours, fruits, honey, etc., is the art of the liqueurist—for in obtaining this balance is the secret of success, frequently unrepeatable with similar ingredients from a different source.

Perhaps the most important decision is the balance between alcoholic strength and sweetness. The former may be strongly influenced by the spirit duty levied by governments, which has a fantastic effect on the eventual consumer price. The latter is influenced by ' trends '—the last decade has shown definite movement towards ' dry '—a relative term, of course, but also influenced from the snob angle, it being said that it is lower income groups who prefer ' sweet ' products and that the higher the income group, the ' drier ' the selection.

MACERATION (INFUSION) is the extraction with cold spirit of soluble products from natural products (usually dried) until equilibrium is attained, and no further extraction takes place. The nature of the materials extracted may vary from a given mixture of raw materials, depending upon the concentration (and temperature) of alcohol in the solvent solution, and this may be specially controlled by the distiller who may wish to extract particular products and leave others. The mixture is usually pulverised to attain maximum extraction. After maceration, the solvent is filtered gently. The filtrate, known as the aromatic infusion, may then be concentrated or even distilled. It may also be mixed with other products (compounded). The final stages of compounding and preparation for bottling are described later.

DIGESTION is maceration in warm solvent and usually the temperature is maintained at 40–50° C. (sometimes 60° C.) for a period of several days. Extraction is far more rapid, and more compounds are liable to be extracted than the cold method. Sometimes the extracted products are removed by steam distillation from the mother liquors.

PERCOLATION

This is a more efficient method of extraction than maceration and may be thought of as 'intensive maceration.' Pure spirit is the solvent at all times which is passed through the natural product and therefore extracts larger quantities of soluble products than maceration. There are two practical methods possible, either continuous passage of pure spirit (cold or hot) through a column or container of the natural product, which requires large quantities of spirit, or a 'closed cycle,' where a constant amount of spirit is heated to boiling point and the condensed vapours pass through the natural products extracting the soluble components. This solution then returns into the boiling solvent and the cycle continues.

This method is, of course, only suitable when the extracted compounds are stable to heat although the solvent temperature can be lowered by using a system working at reduced pressure. The concentrated extracted products are obtained by evaporation of the spirit solvent.

Extraction by percolation is therefore more efficient than maceration, where an equilibrium position of components can be attained between solid and solution. The selection of the method of extraction is totally dependent on the nature, solubility and stability of the compounds to be extracted.

DISTILLATION is the separation of volatile compounds from non-volatile components (tannins, colouring materials, acids, etc.), although the latter may, in small part, be carried over with volatile compounds, particularly alcohol.

Distillation may be carried out under vacuum conditions which lower the temperature of distillation, and thus protects any delicate herbs, etc., which may be temperature sensitive. Either method of distillation, of course, allows definite fractions of distillate to be collected, and in many instances this ' fractionation ' can be of the utmost importance —a small fraction is perfect, whereas the total distillate can be quite useless.

In any distillation process, there are three main fractions of importance.

The first is impure product of low alcoholic strength.

The second is the middle fraction, where quality and strength can be controlled by the rate of heating the still, the pressure of the system (normal atmospheric or vacuum conditions), and whether the fraction is again subdivided with a fractionating column.

The last fraction will be low strength again, and usually useless.

The distillates, of course, are generally water-white, although some may have a very slight colour tinge. The alcoholic strength is high and the distillate is dry. It is therefore necessary to sweeten and colour the distillate to make it into an acceptable liqueur (certain fruit distillates, *kirsch*, *quetsch*, etc., remain dry and colourless, but are reduced in alcoholic strength with pure water). Frequently, additions are made at this stage using herb and spice extracts to add finesse, flavour and harmony to the product.

RECTIFICATION of spirits is the purification by redistillation, which removes aldehydes, fusel oils and other impurities. Before redistillation the spirit is reduced with water in which potash salts have been dissolved.

PREPARATION USING EXTRACTS, ETHEREAL OILS, ETC.

Manufacture by mixing ethereal oils and other dissolved herb and spice extracts with the selected spirit (gin, grain spirit, brandy, whisky, etc.), is the simplest and most reproduceable method of liqueur manufacture. Some schools believe that such liqueurs are second class and that the finest liqueurs need the finesse of distillation and gentle maturing. Modern science, however, enables liqueurists to reproduce these effects without the additional expense involved and more and more modern liqueurs use this technique.

COMPOUNDING

Most liqueurs are produced from a mixture of in-gredients which themselves are obtained by the methods previously described. The compounder will have exact instructions of qualities and quantities of materials and the precise method of mixing. It is not generally realized, and I certainly did not believe it until it happened in my own experiments, that the sequence of mixing is of utmost importance and, by changing a sequence, completely different and apparently inexplicable products can be obtained. Inter-action of materials is obviously causing this, but temperature differences may also give unwanted results. It must also be realised that the alcoholic solvent may affect the compounding operation and if whisky is taken as an example, it must be remembered that no two whiskies will have exactly the same acidity, and this variation of a seemingly minor point has an immense effect on the final product; a change of alcoholic solvent may necessitate a complete revision of the liqueur's formula and compounding operation.

No two compounding operations are identical, and it is the skill of the individual which brings results and continuity of flavour from these operations. In practice, it is essential to demonstrate each operation in a compounding cycle in order to achieve exactly the desired results. The final steps in any compounding operation are sweetening and maturing of the product.

Before a liqueur is ready for marketing, the various ingredients must be given time to marry together to form a single smooth product, rather than a mixture of many flavours lacking in harmony and delicacy. To bring this about requires time, and the following methods are known and have been tried to short circuit ' time ':

Heat   Electrolysis
Ozonisation   Catalytic methods
Movement
Light waves

None of the above methods have really produced acceptable results, and there appears to be no substitute for the age-old method of slow marriage and maturing in oak casks in a warehouse at a uniform cool temperature. The pores of the wooden casks allow slight uptake of air which is essential to ' marriage ' and possibly some of the flavour changes and transformations which are so essential to mellowing and maturing the liqueur.

Wood maturing is most important for whisky liqueurs and any other liqueurs made with flavour-containing spirits where these flavours must themselves combine and mellow with the added flavours of the distiller.

The liqueur may contain colloidal materials which cannot be removed by simple filtration, and a ' fining ' must often be used for clarification and precipitation of the suspension. Most commonly used are albumen, isinglass, white of egg, milk, Spanish earth, bentonite, casein.

Before bottling, the liqueur will be brought to the required alcoholic strength, usually a reduction with water or sugar water, followed by colouring (if necessary) with one of the permitted colouring materials. The finished liqueur will then be bottled after filtration to remove any suspended particles, so that it is crystal clear in its final presentation in the bottle, ready for sale.

Chapter 10

FRUIT LIQUEURS

A CERTAIN amount of confusion exists in the British nomenclature of fruit liqueurs, which is now subject to a code of practice but no definite legal requirements.

The code may be summarised as follows:
" The description 'brandy' or 'fruit brandy' should only be applied to potable spirits derived from the fermented juice of fresh grapes or from the distillation of the fermented juice of other fruits." This definition covers *eaux-de-vie*, which are discussed in Chapter 12.

The terms 'Cherry Brandy,' 'Apricot Brandy' and 'Peach Brandy' are established names for sweet liqueurs made from cherries, apricots and peaches respectively, but *not* by the method stated above, nor are these products *eaux-de-vie*. It is, however, agreed that these two terms may be used for these liqueurs, *provided* that 20% of the spirit content is brandy as defined above.

In the U.S.A., fruit liqueurs made by maceration of fruit in spirit and subsequent sweetening are called 'Cordials.' The distilled dry spirits are called 'Fruit Brandies.' There is no confusion when these terms are correctly applied. In the U.K., however, 'Cordials' are flavoured drinks which can be non-alcoholic or of low alcoholic strength.

Fruit Liqueurs

These can be classified by their three methods of manufacture:

(a) Fruit juice plus spirit—a straightforward compounding operation.

(b) Maceration or percolation of the fruit with a selected spirit followed by slight additional compounding to highlight the flavour. With Stone Fruits it is normal to include the kernel in the primary process. The product may be sweetened or coloured. This is the most usual manufacturing process.

(c) Distillation of the fermented mash of the fruit (with kernels) to produce the dry distilled ' Eau-de-Vie,' Fruit Brandy.

General Classification of Fruits
Apples, pears.

Stone Fruit.—Apricots, cherries, plums (different varieties), nectarines, peaches.

Berries.—Strawberries, raspberries, blackberries, blackcurrants and other berries.

Nuts.—Various edible nuts, coconut.

Citrus Fruit.—Oranges, curaçao oranges, lemons, grapefruit, mandarin.

Tropical and other fruits.—Pineapples, bananas, dates, figs, passion fruit.

Cherry Liqueurs

CERASELLA

One of the finest Italian Cherry Liqueurs supposedly the favourite of the immortal d'Annunzio. The red liqueur has

1. *Peeling oranges for Curaçao production.*

2. *Casks used for maturing Bénédictine.*

3. *Blackcurrant harvest near Dijon.*

4. *Examination of blackcurrants (Cassis production).*

a fine cherry flavour, due to the use of certain digestive herbs from the Abruzzi mountains, which give the liqueur a richness of flavour and unique quality.

HEERING'S CHERRY BRANDY

Until recently known as *Cherry Heering*, this is Danish and is the best known and most widely distributed imported *cherry brandy*.

Starting from a small corner shop 150 years ago, Peter Heering established not only large sales for his special *cherry brandy*, but also became a shipowner of importance—an ideal combination.

The company is still family owned. The shape of the bottle was changed from a characteristic long-necked ' brandy ' shape to the more popular dump ' Bénédictine ' shape, but has now reverted to the original design.

BRITISH CHERRY BRANDIES

These are extremely fine products. *Grant's Morella Cherry Brandy* has been made from brandy and Kent cherries for over 100 years. It is lighter in texture than the imported liqueurs.

The Grants were originally a Scottish family moving South to Sutton Valence. A descendant of these Grants was the originator of their present *cherry brandy*. Destruction of their Dover distillery necessitated a move to Maidstone, where their *cherry brandy* and other liqueurs, including *cherry whisky*, are produced to this day. It is of special interest that through the representations of a great-grandson of the founder, it became possible under the Finance Act 1933 for British compounders to compete ' under bond ' with overseas producers.

Lamb & Watt of Liverpool produce a fine *cherry brandy* in the Danish style, within a range of liqueurs marketed under the brand ' Palatinate,' and another excellent U.K. produced *cherry brandy* is ' *Trotosky* '—a brand also used for other liqueurs.

Cherry liqueurs are produced in many countries and by very many manufacturers. The French *cherry brandies* are usually light in colour and texture. (*Rocher* is well known; *Cherry Marnier* is delicious). *Guignolet* is a term for French *cherry liqueurs*.

The Dutch produce many fine types as do, of course, the Italian and Balkan producers, whose products in the main are produced from dark cherries, giving a heavier liqueur.

ROTE KIRSCH

A deep red, bitter-sweet German *Cherry liqueur* made by Mampe.

KIRSCH PEUREUX

A sweet, water white French *cherry liqueur* quite different from *Kirsch* (see page 46).

VISHNYOVAYA NALIVKA (*Russian cherry liqueur*)

There are several Russian liqueurs produced by in-fusions of cherries, blackberries, blackcurrants and prunes.

Other Russian liqueurs are made on a similar basis to the standard West European types—a liqueur made from cara-way, coriander and lemon is a sweet kümmel type. Coffee, cherry and chocolate liqueurs are made, as are honey-sweetened liqueurs containing roots and grasses, as well as herbs and spices.

NASTOIKAS are sweetened and flavoured brandies.

NALIVKAS are sweet fruit brandies.

WÌSNIAK or WÌSNIÓWKA

Polish *cherry liqueurs*. The latter, which is *vodka* based, is drier.

CHERRY WHISKIES

These have not proved as popular as *cherry brandies*. *Chesky*, made by Frémy, is French. Ross of Leith produce an excellent example better known abroad than at home. Savermo's *Cherry Whiskey* produced in Eire from Irish Whiskey and Czechoslovakian cherries, is no longer available. Other excellent *Scotch cherry whiskies* have been produced as trials, but not as yet marketed. There are certain compounding difficulties in blending the acidities of cherries and Scotch whisky which, when surmounted, will produce liqueurs on a par with Europe's best.

MARASCHINO

A sweet, water white liqueur with a highly concentrated flavour. It is produced from the distillation of fermented maraschino cherries, and their crushed kernels; this variety of cherry being particularly sour, it is thought that sugar is added before fermentation; the distillate may be perfumed with Neroli or with flower blossom extracts. Because of its intense, yet elegant flavour, *maraschino* is a very popular addition to many sweets—fruit salads, jellies, trifles and sorbets.

It is over 200 years ago since Francesco Drioli manufactured his *maraschino* in Zara, then in the Republic of Venice. He introduced the classic maraschino bottle, with its straw casing. Pre-war, the three best known firms, Drioli,

Luxardo and Magazzin, manufactured in Zara in Dalmatia, centre for the amarasca, the best cherries for their liqueurs. This district is now part of Yugoslavia and although *maraschino* is still made there, Drioli is now made in Venice and Luxardo in Padua.

Many cherry liqueurs are given extra finesse and elegance by the addition of approximately 2% *eaux-de-vie*, usually *kirsch*. This small quantity is sufficient to lift the bouquet and introduce high flavour tones which quite change the character of the liqueur, giving delicacy which can change a dull product into an excellent one.

APRICOT LIQUEURS

Every Continental, British and American liqueur producer includes an *apricot liqueur* in his range. The majority are made by maceration of ripe apricots with grape brandy frequently with the addition of kernel extracts or *eaux-de-vie*. Best known are the ' *Abricotine* ' of the French firm of Garnier (whose famous distillery is at Enghien-les-Bains and who are specialists in fancy pack production and novelty bottles), Marie Brizard's ' *Apry* ' and the Dutch *Bols Apricot Brandy*.

The word *brandy* in connection with apricot (and peach and cherry liqueurs) is, strictly speaking, a misnomer. True *Apricot Brandy* is the distilled product of fermented apricots and their kernels, a white high-strength dry *eau-de-vie*. Best known is the Hungarian *Barack Palinka*. It is also made in other East European countries.

PEACH LIQUEURS

These are made by very many manufacturers and are normally sweet and rich, produced by maceration or percolation of ripe peaches in spirit. To obtain the best flavour, extracts of the peach kernel are essential and it is not unknown for *eaux-de-vie* to be added to increase the delicacy of the bouquet.

SOUTHERN COMFORT

A much esteemed *whiskey liqueur* from the U.S.A., made from a base of Bourbon with peach flavouring and fresh peaches and oranges. It is drunk neat or in numerous mixed drinks.

SOFT FRUIT LIQUEURS

BLACKBERRY LIQUEURS

(a) *Sweet Liqueur*, prepared by the maceration of fully ripe blackberries in brandy or spirit. The product may require sweetening and *eaux-de-vie* is frequently added to give finesse to the liqueur. The liqueur is made by several European producers; the Polish variety is called *Jerzynowka*.

A particularly fine German liqueur is made from the Kroatzbeere, which is similar to the blackberry. It is deep purple, not too sweet with the wonderful bouquet of the wild blackberry.

(b) Dry distilled *blackberry brandy*.

See *Eaux-de-vie*, page 48.

RASPBERRY LIQUEUR, CRÈME DE FRAMBOISES

Made by the same process as *blackberry liqueurs*, using fully ripe raspberries. Pagès make an interesting pink ' *Framboise Sauvage* ' from wild raspberries grown in Southwest France.

A particularly fine example with a delicious bouquet is made in Holland by Cooymans.

STRAWBERRY LIQUEUR, CRÈME DE FRAISES

Strawberry liqueur made from fully ripe strawberries by the same methods as blackberry and raspberry liqueurs.

CRÈME DE FRAISES DES BOIS

Liqueur made from wild strawberries.

CASSIS is a French liqueur produced by addition of sugar to macerated blackcurrants in alcohol or *eau-de-vie*. Addition of up to 5% raspberries and redcurrants is permitted. additional colouring is forbidden.

BLACKCURRANT LIQUEUR, CRÈME DE CASSIS

This has been known for centuries, and as early as the sixteenth century monks in the Dijon area (where the finest blackcurrants grow) produced a blackcurrant ratafia to which many remedial properties were attributed, particularly against current physical diseases. The berries are rich in Vitamin C and the liqueur is a healthy and enjoyable *digestif*.

The liqueur is made by macerating the destalked blackcurrants in grape brandy. It is sweet, red and full flavoured. A blended liqueur of blackcurrants and others is marketed by Bols as Bolsberry Liqueur. In Eastern Europe the liqueur was called *Bocksbeeren*.

SLOE GIN—the traditional ' Stirrup cup ' of Old England. It is a rich, deep-red liqueur made by steeping ripe unblemished sloe berries (the fruit of the blackthorn bush) in gin. Other fruits may occasionally be added to increase the flavour, depending upon the quality of the crop. The liqueur is matured in wood, and the finished liqueur has valuable astringent properties, good for the digestion.

Pedlar brand made by Hawkers of Plymouth, who have supplied the Royal Household for 300 years, is best known of the British *sloe gins*—their ' gold label ' is de luxe quality made from hand-picked sloes in the best years; others are produced by Ross of Leith and Lamb & Watt.

CRÈME DE PRUNELLE

French and Dutch liqueurs made from plums occasionally with the addition of a small quantity of other stone fruit, including kernels.

For *plum brandies*, see ' *Eaux-de-Vie*,' page 47.

FINNISH LIQUEURS

The land of the midnight sun produces wonderful liqueurs from otherwise little-known native fruits. There are three main liqueurs produced by Lignell and Piispanen and others:

KARPI

This is a fine aromatic liqueur made from cranberries (karpalo) and other bitter-sweet wild-growing berries from Finland's marshlands (where the fruits are also enjoyed by bears!) The fruit is often snow-covered before the end of the harvest, in which case it is picked in the spring.

SUOMUURAIN

This is made only from cloudberries (Rubus Chamae-morus) grown in the Arctic North. The berries are picked during the mild spring weather, and the susceptibility of the tree to sudden frost during flowering has caused the loss of many a year's crop and has thus limited the production of this very fine and delicately flavoured bitter-sweet liqueur. The liqueur is sometimes called *Lakka*.

MESIMARJA LIQUEUR

Also known as the ' Red Pearl of the North.' It is a truly delightfully aromatic liqueur made from the Arctic Bramble (Rubus Arcticus).

Other Fruit Liqueurs

CRÈME D'ANANAS, PINEAPPLE LIQUEUR

An excellent golden pineapple liqueur on *rum* base is made by Lamb & Watt, and obtains its special flavour by long maturing in wooden casks. A Hawaiian type is available in the U.S.A., and a Dutch variety, *Tornado*, is made by Hulstkamp from an old recipe based on Hawaiian fruit.

CRÈME DE BANANE, BANANA LIQUEUR

A sweet yellow liqueur made by maceration of ripe bananas in pure spirit. The liqueur usually has a very strong banana bouquet and is made in many countries, including Australia.

Mus is a Turkish brand.

NEZHINSKAYA RYAFINA

Sweet Russian rowan flavoured brandies with a sharp taste.

RABINOWKA

Another form of *rowanberry liqueur* from Eastern countries; imported pre-war from Riga.

SABRA

A mild, red bitter-sweet liqueur made in Israel from the hardy desert sabra cactus. This fruit grows in the Mediterranean region of Africa, and is found in rocky desert land. Presentation is in a reproduction of a Phoenician jug. However the flavour has now been changed to orange and chocolate.

ZOLOTAYA OSEN (Golden Autumn)

Caucasian damson, apple and quince liqueur; bitter-sweet.

There are many German liqueurs such as ' *Kirsch mit Whisky*,' ' *Aprikose mit Whisky*,' etc., which are fruit liqueurs based on spirit and whisky; the latter may be local whisky or partly imported whisky. If the whisky origin is not stated in any form, it may be assumed to be local produce.

Chapter 11

CITRUS LIQUEURS

CURAÇAO

THE original orange curaçao was made with fruit from the Island of Curaçao, but the term has become generic and is also used for liqueurs made from oranges of other origins.

The flesh of the orange is discarded, only the peel being used, and it is most important that the oranges be gathered at the correct time. The fine flavours are extracted by soaking in water, then steeping in spirit followed by distillation, and rectification. Many Dutch distillers import dried orange peel from Curaçao, which has retained the essential oils and other flavour compounds.

Excellent *curaçaos* are made by Bols and Fockink in Holland and by most French producers, and they are available in many colours, orange, brown, white, blue and green. Visitors to Amsterdam should not miss a visit to Wynand Fockink's Tasting Room with its unique atmosphere and delightful drinking ceremony where a range of *curaçaos* and other liqueurs can be enjoyed. *TRIPLE-SEC WHITE CURAÇAO* is water-white, highly rectified *curaçao*; see page 18.

COINTREAU is the most popular of the triple-sec *curaçaos*. Because of imitations of the bottle and the label before the war, the brand name 'Cointreau' replaced the old title 'Triple-sec,' which was, and still is, used by other distillers.

The House of Cointreau was founded in 1849 and continues to produce fine liqueurs at Angers using the delicious fruits of Anjou in their preparation, marketed under the Regnier label (U.K.) and Cointreau brand (U.S.A.).

GRAND MARNIER is one of the best known Curaçao which is made at Neauphle-le-Château and at Château-de-Bourg. The manufacturing company, Ets. Marnier-Lapostolle, was founded in 1827 and from modest beginnings the company grew until, in 1880, Grand Marnier was invented based on Cognac and distinguished by the fact that the spirit base is exclusively Cognac. The subtle bouquet is produced by distillation of the orange steeped in Cognac and the excellent blending of the liqueur produces a superb, inimitable masterpiece. Two qualities are marketed—Cordon Rouge and Cordon Jaune, the latter of lower strength.

AURUM

A golden fruit and herb liqueur based on the orange, but spiked with the pungent peel,' produced at Pescara, Italy. The spirit is old brandy, and all the ingredients are harvested in the Abruzzi mountains.

POMERANZEN LIQUEURS

Mainly German liqueurs of the Curaçao type based on unripe Pomeranzen oranges; green and orange, sometimes called gold.

HALB UND HALB, HALF-OM-HALF

German and Dutch liqueurs, usually an equal blend of orange *curaçao* and orange *bitters*.

VAN DER HUM is a South African liqueur made from an orange-type fruit—the Naartjies, and flavoured with other fruits, plants, seeds and barks. Whilst there is no exact record of the origins, it is obvious that the Dutch settlers made this liqueur in imitation of their well loved Curaçao. The name Van der Hum arose from settlers being unable to remember the name of the inventor, and is in translation, " Mr. What's his name." Although Bertrams has been made for 100 years, and is the best known, there are many fine Van der Hums produced.

CRÈME DE MANDARINE (TANGERINE)

Liqueurs obtained from the dried peel of tangerine similar to Curaçao's production from oranges. Dutch and French varieties are excellent from various producers; the Danish ' San Michele ' is particularly well known.

FORBIDDEN FRUIT is an old American liqueur with a fine citrus flavour and bitter-sweet tang originating from the Shaddock (which is an unusual fruit of the grapefruit family) blended seductively with honey and orange. The liqueur was served and popularized by Del Monico in New York. It has been said that this liqueur was so good that it was ' Nectar of the Gods—forbidden to man.' The liqueur is marketed in a uniquely attractive orb shaped bottle decorated with gilt filigree.

LEMON LIQUEUR is a typical citrus liqueur. The citron variety is rich in essential oils, which give flavours to the liqueur; also added are extracts of flower petals and oil of Neroli. The citron of Mampe-Berlin is delicious. Some *lemon* liqueurs are marketed as *Bergamot Liqueur*, the name of a special lemon variety grown in Mediterranean countries to produce Bergamot oil for the perfumery industry. The Austrian variety is confusingly called *kaiserbirnlikör*.

CITRONEN-EIS LIKÖR is a yellow German liqueur made from lemon juice and lemon peel distillate, intended for drinking ' on-the-rocks.'

KITRON, Greek spirit obtained by distillation of grape brandy with leaves of lemon trees. The product may be sweetened into a liqueur.

CAYO VERDE, an American liqueur, light in texture, made from key limes and spirit.

FILFAR is a curaçao type liqueur made in Cyprus. It is often bottled in stone jugs.

MERSIN, Turkish triple-sec curaçao, named after the port on the south coast of Turkey.

PARFAIT AMOUR is an exotic, sweet citrus-oil based liqueur. It is scented and is slightly spiced and is very similar to *Crème de Violettes* with additional flavour from flower petals. It is made in several colours, mainly bright violet, by most major European producers.

PASSION FRUIT LIQUEUR is a deep golden sweet citrus flavoured liqueur made in Australia. A brand is Grand Cumberland.

CAPRICORNIA is another Australian liqueur made from Tropical fruits.

ROCK AND RYE, American liqueur; made by steeping citrus and other fruits in rye whiskey. The name is derived from the original liqueur, which was rock candy crystallized on the sides of the bottle and rye whiskey.

Chapter 12

FRUIT BRANDIES

EAUX-DE-VIE (' *Waters of Life* ')

These are dry fruit brandies usually bottled at higher alcoholic strength (approx. 45° GL = 79° proof) than liqueurs and infrequently aged before bottling.

CALVADOS (*Applejack*)

This is apple brandy, which takes its name from the town of Calvados, the Normandy centre of the French apple orchards.

Calvados is romantically linked with the Vikings, and when the Norsemen took over Normandy over 1,000 years ago, they found rich farmlands and apple orchards and soon discovered the pleasure of apple alcohol.

Legend has it that in the eleventh century, the Normans enjoyed a glass of *calvados* in the middle of a meal, which not only facilitated digestion, but also sharpened the appetite for greater enjoyment of the remainder of the meal. Such enjoyable customs are, of course, handed down from generation to generation, and it became known as the ' *Trou Normand* '— the Norman hole making space for further food. As an appetizer, it should be tossed back in one gulp—as a brandy or apéritif ' on-the-rocks ' it should be slowly sipped.

Fully ripe apples are crushed and fermented with cultured yeast and the mash pot-distilled to produce low wines which are then redistilled to produce *calvados* of high strength. Maturing in oak casks is essential and ' *Un Trou Normand* '—one of the finest—is at least six years old before bottling, and is golden brown, the colour obtained from its slow maturing in the wooden casks.

All *calvados* must be submitted to a tasting committee, and before a Certificate of Quality is granted allowing the brandy sample to be called ' *calvados*,' it must pass scrutiny of experts, who jealously guard the reputation of their Normandy brandy.

In the U.S.A., ' *applejack* ' is made similarly, but it is generally marketed younger than *calvados*.

EAUX-DE-VIE-DE-CIDRE (de-Poiré)

Fruit spirit obtained by distillation of cider (*apple wine*) or perry (*pear wine*).

POIRE WILLIAMS

The *eau-de-vie* produced by distilling the fermented juice of the Williams Pear. This brandy is often sold in a pear-shaped bottle containing a ripe pear, which was grown in the bottle as it hangs on the tree.

The Swiss producers frequently age the pear brandy in wooden casks, after which it is bottled at high strength.

Produced in Switzerland, Alsace and Provence and Germany.

KIRSCH, QUETSCH AND OTHER STONE FRUIT BRANDIES

It is essential to include crushed kernels in the fruit juice which is fermented and twice distilled in pot-stills, as they give a fine bitter tang to the brandy. The water-white brandies cannot be aged in wood, as this would give them colour. The fragrance of the fruit brandies is preserved by bottling soon after distillation at fairly high strength or by storage in large glass containers.

EAU-DE-VIE de:

Kirsch= Cherry; *prune*= Plum; *quetsch*= Switzen Plum; *mirabelle*=Mirabelle Plum.

KIRSCHWASSER

This is the German Black Forest speciality, whose special quality is attributed to the site, the soil and the selection of the cherry type. The name—wasser (water) is surely a misnomer for high strength dry flavoured spirit!

Utmost importance in the manufacture of a fine product is stressed on rapid distillation after the end of the fermentation of the fruit mash, as all fruit wines are readily spoiled by acetobacter (bacteria which turn alcohol to vinegar). Fruit brandies, *kirsch* in particular, are frequently added to sweet fruit liqueurs to add finesse, elegance and bouquet.

PLUM BRANDIES

Mirabelle and swizten plums are the basis of excellent flavoursome brandies, produced on the same principle as *kirsch*, called *mirabelle* and *quetsch* (*Zwetschenwasser* or *Zwetgenwasser*) respectively. Both are water-white, bottled at high strength and produced in France, Germany, Switzerland and in many Balkan countries, where they are collectively called *slivovitz* (*slivovica* in Yugoslavia, *slibovitza* in Rumania). The latter uniquely may be cask matured when, naturally, some colour may be taken up.

Serbian plum and juniper brandy is called *klekovaca;* Rumanian plum brandy with almond flavour is *tzuica.*

APRICOT BRANDY
See page 36.

SOFT FRUIT BRANDIES (*Eaux-de-Vie*)
Very fine delicately flavoured brandies are produced from soft fruit—raspberries, strawberries, blackberries, etc.

With all fruit brandies, it is absolutely essential to control the fermentation temperature—low temperature slows the fermentation, too high a temperature will lose bouquet and flavour and the range 20°-22°C. is considered best.

EAU-DE-VIE de:
Framboise—raspberry—France, Germany, Switzerland (Himbeergeist).

Fraise—strawberry—France, Germany, Switzerland (Erdbeergeist).

Fraises de Bois—wild strawberry—France, Germany, Switzerland.

Blackberry—France, Germany, Switzerland (Brombeergeist).

Fig—Morocco and other Mediterranean countries.

German nomenclature differentiates between fruit brandies termed *-wasser* and *-geist.*

"*Wasser*" (e.g. *Kirschwasser*) are produced by distillation of the fermented fruit mash.

"*Geist*" (e.g. *Himbeergeist*) are produced by maceration of the fruit in alcohol followed by distillation. This method is essential for soft fruits with a low sugar content.

German apple and pear brandies are classified as '*Branntwein.*'

5. *Vve. Champion Distillery, Bordeaux, in the 1890's.*

6. *Stillroom, Cusenier Distillery, Marseilles.*

7. *Glen Mist returns to Scotland, 1963. The author adding one of the secret ingredients.*

Chapter 13

HERB LIQUEURS

DRAMBUIE

THE oldest and most famous whisky liqueur, it is based on a private recipe originating from Prince Charles Edward Stuart, Bonnie Prince Charlie. Legend has it that after the unsuccessful eighteenth century rebellion, the '45, when the Scottish Rebels were completely defeated at the battle of Culloden Moor, it was one of his Highland friends, Mackinnon of Strathaird, who gave shelter to the hunted Prince, and successfully found him transport to France. As a mark of personal gratitude and affection, the Prince is said to have presented his personal recipe to Mackinnon, whose family still to this day produce and market it as *Drambuie*— the gaelic for 'the drink that satisfies.'

GLEN MIST, SCOTCH WHISKY LIQUEUR

In terms of ancient recipes, *Glen Mist* is young, but nevertheless, it is the second oldest of all whisky liqueurs, invented by Hector MacDonald. It is now produced again, by the author in Scotland after its eighteen year excursion to Eire. At the beginning of the war, the recipe was purchased by Savermo Ltd., who appointed S. F. & O. Hallgarten as sole distributors for their *Glen Mist*. When Scotch whisky

49

supplies became impossible, and honey and sugar unobtainable in austerity England of 1945, production was taken to Eire by S. F. Hallgarten, until it returned to Scotland in 1963. While it was made in Eire, the base was Irish whiskey. During this period, world-wide export and English supplies were directed from Eire, and in order to avoid marketing misunderstanding, parallel to *Glen Mist* production, another liqueur was created—*Irish Mist*. A third much drier liqueur, ' *Whisqueur,*' was produced during the period when Scotch whisky was in short supply.

Glen Mist is a blend of herbs, spices, honey and only the finest fully matured Scotch whisky is used as its base. The liqueur is matured in whisky casks for a long time, and is totally produced and bottled in Scotland. Of the three Scotch liqueurs internationally marketed, *Glen Mist* is the driest and is, therefore, much appreciated by connoisseurs of good food and drink.

In the U.S.A., where the term ' Scotch Whisky Liqueur ' means a half-bottle of Scotch whisky (slightly sweetened), *Glen Mist* is marketed as ' Scotland's Finest Liqueur.'

GLAYVA

A herb and spice liqueur, produced after the war by Ronald Morrison in Scotland.

CLANRANA

A modern liqueur made in Scotland.

CAN-Y-DELYN

A modern liqueur inspired by the mountains and valleys of Wales.

DEWMIEL

A modern Scotch whisky liqueur.

LINDISFARNE LIQUEUR

An English liqueur made on a whisky base with honey.

IRISH MIST LIQUEUR

A herb and honey liqueur based on Irish whiskey developed by the liqueur company originally created in Eire together with Irish interests by Savermo Ltd., and its managing director, S. F. (Fritz) Hallgarten, during the time when *Glen Mist* production was transferred to Tullamore.

BÉNÉDICTINE

About the year 1510 the learned monk, Don Bernardo Vincelli, at Fécamp, is said to have discovered this great elixir which, when consumed in modest quantities, revived the tired monks.

The elixir was used to combat malarial diseases prevalent in the countryside around the monastery, no doubt a most popular medicine with fishermen and peasants alike. In 1534, Francis I, King of France, visited the monastery and praised the elixir which was known as ' *Bénédictine ad majorem Dei gloriam* '—' Bénédictine for the greater glory of God.' The Fécamp Abbey was destroyed during the French revolution and the order dispersed. The recipe, however, was entrusted to the *Procureur Fiscal* of the Abbey and later came into the hands of Monsieur Alexandre le Grand, a wine merchant and descendant of the original trustee.

The recipe was successfully used to reconstruct the original liqueur and this fine liqueur is now shipped to many countries, each bottle bearing the title D.O.M.—' *Deo Optimo Maximo* '—' To God most good, most great.'

It interested me to hear that large quantities are shipped to Malaysia, where it is very popular with Chinese workers in the tin mines, who spend hours knee-deep in water at their work. Tradition has it that *Bénédictine* helps prevent rheumatism and other muscular aches!

51

B. & B.

Bénédictine and *Brandy* is a drier version of *Bénédictine* and more to the current popular taste, particularly in North America.

CHARTREUSE

The Carthusian order was founded by St. Bruno almost 900 years ago, at Chartreuse, near Grenoble in the French Alps. Over the centuries, the monastery was rebuilt several times, usually following destruction by fire, and the present building at Voiron is almost 300 years old. The production of a liqueur was unknown until 1848, when a group of army officers quartered at the monastery, were offered a liqueur as *digestif* after dinner. Needless to say, it was found to be extraordinarily fine and they promised to spread word of the discovery. Demand increased rapidly, so that by 1860, it was necessary to build a distillery at Fourvoirie to cope with it. At the turn of the century in 1903, the Carthusians were expelled from France, and continued to make their liqueur in Tarragona, where they found refuge, until their return to France in 1931. During exile they advertised ' *Demandez une Tarragone* ' and pointed out that the liqueur was the same, only the bottle being different.

I recently tasted a bottle of Chartreuse which was approximately 100 years old. The dark green bottle was etched with the name, but without indication of strength. The liqueur was pale yellow, not dissimilar from today's product, surprisingly enough with less herbal flavour and spicier alcohol tones—a delicious tasting experience.

Chartreuse is marketed at two strengths: 96° proof (green) and 75° proof (yellow). Imitations abound but although many are of similar type and character, none can equal the flavour and finesse of the original recipe of the Carthusian monks. There was a time, however, when licence was granted to manufacture Chartreuse; but unfortunately, there are no records available about this arrangement, neither the quantity produced nor the distribution achieved.

There are many French, and other Chartreuse imitations, liqueurs jaunes and liqueurs vertes. Many of the French ones are localised and I recall tasting an excellent brand, *Grignan* (79° proof) in the Rhône-Ventoux region, which is made by Trappist monks.

German imitations are generically named '*Kartauser,*' The imitations of *Bénédictine* are called *Diktiner*. *Monastique* is a similar liqueur.

CORDIAL MÉDOC is a flavoury sweet red liqueur based on old claret flavoured with herb extracts. It is produced in Bordeaux.

IZARRA (*Basque for Star*).

Izarra is produced in two forms—green (85° proof) and yellow (64° proof). It has been made since 1835 from an old recipe. Production is on an *Armagnac* base with flavouring drawn from plants grown in the French Pyrenees.

TRAPPISTINE

A very old formula in the possession of the Monks of the Abbey of Grace-Dieu, in France, is still used to produce

Trappistine. The liqueur, which is pale green-yellow, is produced from freshly gathered herbs from the Doubs mountains and is based on *Armagnac*. It is sold in characteristically shaped bottles at 75° proof.

LA VIEILLE CURE

This liqueur has been produced at the Abbey of Cenon, in the Gironde district, since mediaeval times. It is made from a secret formula, whose preparation entails maceration of fifty root and aromatic plants in Armagnac and Cognac.

FIOR D'ALPI (*Flower of the Alps*)

There are several fine Italian herb liqueurs; one of the best—' *Mille Fiori*,' which is assumed to contain extracts from a thousand flowers—is made by Distilleria Vigevanese, who have been distillers and compounders for more than ninety years. Others are called *Isolabella* and *Edelweiss*.

The liqueurs are presented in tall white flute bottles containing a ' Christmas Tree ' made of a small twig on which hang crystals of sugar. The liqueurs are smooth and reviving. Certain difficulties are experienced with importation as the actual contents of bottles varies, as does the alcoholic strength due to the liqueur being bottled when warm and containing large amounts of sugar which crystallize on the twig as the liqueur slowly cools.

GALLIANO

A golden yellow Italian herb liqueur in a very tall distinctive flute bottle named after Major Giuseppe Galliano, who, against heavy odds, halted the army of Menelik at Enda Jesus in the Italian Abyssinian war (1895/96) and was thus instrumental in ending the war.

STREGA

According to legend, beautiful maidens disguised as witches once mixed a magic drink in the city of Benevento. Tradition decrees that when two people taste this drink they are for ever united.

Strega is a neutral yellow Italian liqueur made from the flavours of over seventy herbs and barks, to a formula which may be centuries old. It is a popular liqueur drunk neat and is very good with ice-cream.

ELIXIR D'ANVERS

A full-flavoured, soft but not too sweet after-dinner liqueur made by de Beukelaer in Antwerp. The herbs and seeds used in the production of this green-yellow liqueur give a fine bitter-sweet flavour. It is still made by the old-fashioned methods to ensure continuity, and is recognised as the Belgian national liqueur.

ELIXIR DE SPA

The town of Spa has been famous as a watering place from the twelfth century, and in the middle ages many Royal Counts visited it to take the Cure.

In 1643, Capuchin Friars took up residence near Spa under the patronage of Walter de Livorlo and these Friars invented an *Elixir* made from distilled extracts of local plants. A sweet liqueur, the *Elixir* was recommended for its tonic and digestive qualities.

The monastery was dissolved in 1797. The formula was, fortunately, found in a manuscript from the old library, and it is still being used for regular production.

HERBS	BRITISH	<u>GLEN MI</u>
	EUROPEAN	Cuaranta-y-tres 55 <u>MILLE FIORJ</u> 70 Partait Amour ▨ French Ponche Soto 56 Dutch 75 Trappistine 70 Aurur
	SEED	44 Anisette Greek Ouzo 65 67 Anis del Mo
	MINT	Dutch ▨ Crème de Menthe ▨ French 50 RO
FRUIT	CITRUS	Van der Hum 54 Orange ▨ Curaçao 52
	APRICOT PEACH	42 Trotosky Apricot Brandy ▨ French Apricot Brandy ▨ ▨ Dutch Apricot Brandy
	CHERRY	Grants Cherry Whisky, Brandy 43 44 50 Scottish Cherry Whisky 52 42 Trotosky ▨ Dutch Cherry Brandy 47 Maraschino 70 Wiśniówk French Cherry Brandy ▨ 43 Cherry Heering
	ARCTIC FRUITS	39 <u>SUOMUURAIN</u>
	MISCELLANEOUS FRUITS	▨ Crème de Cassis Blackberry ▨ ▨ Crème de Fraises (1/6) Pedlar 47 Sloe Gin Blackcurrant Rum Crème de Framboise ▨ ▨ Crème de Banane 52 Pineapple Rum 42
BEAN & KERNEL	COFFEE	Kahlúa 46 55 Tia Maria 60 Gallweys
	CHOCOLATE	Scotch Coffee Whisky 50 ▨ Crème de Cacao 50 RO
	FRUIT KERNEL	52 <u>NOYAU ROSE</u>
SPIRITS	FRUIT (EAUX-DE-VIE)	Polish Slivovltz 70 Tequila 7
	GIN VODKA WHISKY WHISKEY BRANDY	65 British Gin 70 British Vodkas 80 Smirnov Smirnov 65·5 70 Geneva Polish 73 Vodka Wolfschmldt Russian 70 V Scotch Whisky 70 American Whiskey Grape Brandy 70 De Luxe Scot Irish Whiskey
	RUM DARK WHITE	Jamaica, Demerara 70 70 Appleton Estate 90 Car Imperial Diamond 70 70 Daïquiri 70 Ron Bacardi

1973 - 3rd. Edition by Peter Hallgarten

LIQUEU

Liqueurs, Ea

60
70 | 70 | Drambuie

Strega 70 | 73 | Benedictine | 75 | Yellow Chartreuse | Green Chartreuse 96

64 | Yellow Izarra | 73 | B & B | 75 | Vieille Cure

D'ANVERS 66 | Cordial Médoc 70 | 70 | Galliano | 85 | Green Izarra

nod 70 | DANZIG GOLDWASSER 75 | Liqueur d'Or
mmel DER LACHS
LATE

Chocolate Grand Marnier 68 | 70 | Cointreau

8 | Triple Sec | 55.8 | FORBIDDEN FRUIT

Peach Brandy

- Chocolate

Kirsch Peureux 70

Mesimarja 39 | 50 | KARPI

a- Chocolate

LATE

D | Calvados "UN TROU NORMAND"

uavit 100 | Kosher White Spirit | Russian 98 | Krepkaya

CHOLOFF (5 year) Vodka | 100 | Polish Spirit

D | NICHOLOFF RED Vodka

agnac 70 | 70 | STAUB Fine Champagne Cognac | 70 | V.S.O.P Cognac | Liqueur Cognac 70

100 | Woods

EGG LIQUEURS

Advocaat 30° proof, | Dutch, Guernsey

APPROX **PROOF** STRENGTH OF A LIQUEUR TYPE AT VARIOUS STRENGTHS BY SEVERAL DISTILLERS·

70 = 70° PROOF IN BRITISH PROOF (SYKES)

70 British Proof = 80 US Proof = 40% alcohol by volume

---

70 | Kirsch d'Alsace | Framboise 78

Quetsch 78 | Mirabelle 78 | Poire William 75

Polish White Spirit 140

GRAPH ©

d Spirits

Subject to change and correction. E & O E

Published by Wineographs, Highgate Road, London, NW5 1RR

CALISAY

A Spanish liqueur of sweetened spirit flavoured with cinchona and other barks.

CUARANTA-Y-TRES

Spanish herb liqueur made, as its name suggests, from forty-three herbs. It is golden in colour.

SAPINDOR

Liqueur de Sapin is made from plants grown in the Jura mountains. The base is spirit and it has been produced in Pontarlier since 1825. The bottle is shaped and coloured like the bark of a tree—the liqueur is green, pleasantly aromatic with a spicy taste.

BRONTË

A Yorkshire liqueur based on brandy with honey and herb flavouring. Distributed in a characteristic pottery container.

ANGELICA LIQUEUR

Sweet Basque liqueur flavoured with angelica and Pyreneean plants. *Krambambuli* is an East German variety, including violet extracts.

AIGUEBELLE

This was first made at the turn of the nineteenth century in green and yellow forms. Père Hughes discovered the recipe when he found an ancient parchment with ' *Formule de la liqueur de Frère Jean.*' The liqueur is made from over fifty different herbs.

CARLSBERG

A bitter Czechoslovakian liqueur made from selected herbs and selected thermal waters. Also made in West Germany since the war.

CARMELINE

Carmeline was produced in Bordeaux until several years ago. It was a neutral, green-yellow herb liqueur.

CHINA-CHINA

French liqueur made from spices and other flavours.

COCUY

A Venezuelan brandy distilled from fermented sisal roots.

ENZIAN LIQUEURS

Bavarian liqueurs made from mountain gentian plants. A distilled, strongly scented brandy is also made in alpine parts of Germany, France and Switzerland. It is valued medicinally for stomach pains.

ETTALER

German herb liqueurs available, yellow (73° proof) and green (77° proof). They are made in Kloster Ettel, a Benedictine monastery near Oberammergau.

GORNY DOUBNYAK

A Russian bitter liqueur made from an infusion containing oils of ginger, galingale, angelica root, clove, acorns and oak shavings.

GINGER LIQUEURS

Made by maceration of ginger root in pure spirit. A very fine Dutch ginger liqueur is marketed by Berry Bros. and Rudd Ltd., of London, known as 'King's Ginger Liqueur.'

It is golden, dryish with a pronounced spicy ginger bouquet and crisp flavour, and is said to have been a favourite liqueur of King Edward VII.

JÄGERMEISTER
Dark red German herb liqueur.

LIQUEUR DES MOINES
' Liqueur of the Monks '—an excellent yellow digestive produced from aromatic plants and old matured cognac.

MONTE AGUILA
A Jamaican liqueur introduced after the war which is not available generally in the U.K. The liqueur is made from Jamaican ingredients, the dominant flavour is pimento (all-spice). The liqueur is slightly bitter and an excellent digestive.

RASPAIL
A yellow French liqueur, based on herbs, originated by François Raspail in 1847. Raspail is proclaimed as the fore-runner of Pasteur; the former believed that his liqueur would possess digestive and medicinal properties. Although he was not qualified, he was very interested in medical problems, and originally named his liqueur ' Veritable liqueur hygienique et de dessert.' The recipe contains angelica, calamus, myrrh and other interesting natural products. It is still produced at Cenon by a subsidiary of Bols.

LA SENANCOLE
A yellow herb liqueur, aromatic and spicy, made by the monks of the Abbey de Senanque, founded by the Cistercian Order in 1148, at Salon, Provence.

It is recorded that one of the priors, Dom Marie Augustin, used local plants, which grew in abundance and invented a delicately flavoured ' *digestif* ' which he named ' *La Senancole* ' after the river torrent which flows at the foot of the valley below the Abbey. The liqueur has been privately made since 1930, under the supervision of the prior, from the herbs which are still gathered by the monks. It is still to be found in France, particularly in and around Marseilles.

ST. HALLVARD

An interesting golden coloured Norwegian liqueur. It is made from neutral potato spirit subtly flavoured with herbs and aromatic botanicals.

SÈVE

A sweetened orange coloured and flavoured herb liqueur made by Fournier-Demars, at St. Amand (Cher). Other producers also manufacture *Sève* liqueurs based on Cognac or Fine Champagne.

STONSDORFER

Dark German bitter herb liqueur.

TAPIO

A herb and juniper liqueur based on an old Finnish recipe. It is water-white with a good, dry, herbal flavour.

VERVEINE DU VELAY

Two original liqueurs are made by Pagès, in South-west France, green and yellow; both are herb liqueurs with a sharp bitter flavour.

ROYAL GINGER-CHOCOLATE LIQUEUR

Introduced by the author in 1970, it is a completely new and unique flavour combination with the tang of ginger yet smooth and delicate.

Chapter 14

LIQUEURS WITH ONE HERB FLAVOUR PREDOMINATING

ABSINTHE

A PRODUCT now banned, in its original form, in many countries. Historically, *absinthe* was a very dry and bitter spirit of high alcoholic strength made from many aromatic herbs, including aniseed, liquorice, fennel, hyssop, coriander, orris root and wormwood, all of which are grown in the Jura mountains. It was marketed by Henri Louis Pernod, who built a large trade for it until it was banned by France and Switzerland just before the Great War. Imitation *absinthes* are marketed by replacing the dangerous ingredient wormwood with other components such as aniseed.

The most widely distributed *absinthe* substitute is *Pernod Anis*, which, although available at a lower strength than the original, appears to be a similar elixir, and is consumed in identical fashion—dry with water and ice, which turns it milky. In Edwardian days many women found *absinthe* too dry and remedied this by pouring the liqueur dropwise through a lump of sugar perched on a special absinthe spoon.

ANISETTE

Most liqueur compounders produced *aniseed liqueurs*, which are sweetened aniseed on a pure spirit base. The most famous is produced by Marie Brizard, of Bordeaux. Marie Brizard, who was born in 1714, inherited a secret formula for the production of *anisette*, and halfway through the eighteenth century she and her nephew, Jean-Baptiste Roger, manufactured this and other liqueurs commercially. They are now acknowledged as founders of the French liqueur industry. The distillery is still family owned, and their products are world renowned.

ANIS DEL MONO
Spanish aniseed liqueur produced in Barcelona. It is water-white and is made in dry and sweet varieties.

ANISETTA STELLATA
Italian aniseed liqueur produced by the Aurum distillery in Pescara.

ELIXIR DE CHINA
Sweet, water-white Italian aniseed liqueur.

ESCARCHADO
Portuguese aniseed liqueur containing sugar crystals.

LA TINTAINE
A French herb liqueur with a predominating aniseed flavour. It is presented in a bottle with a fennel stem, which gives a tree effect.

MASTIC, MASTICHA
Sweet white Greek and Cypriot liquorice flavoured liqueurs. They are made from aniseed and the sap from trees of the cashew family. One of the finest comes from the Island of Chios.

MASTIKA

Dry Balkan anis liqueur.

OJEN

Spanish absinthe type liqueur.

OUZO

White Greek and Cyprus anisette liqueurs which are drier than the North European types. *Ouzo* is normally drunk on the rocks, when it turns milky with the water. *Douzico* is the Macedonian dialect form of *Ouzo*.

OXYGENÉE

Aniseed-flavoured *absinthe* substitute made in France and U.S.A.

PASTIS (*de Marseilles*)

French aniseed-flavoured liqueurs, the best known is Ricard.

RAKI

Aniseed and liquorice-flavoured Turkish liqueur, drunk with ice and water. The name has become generic for Eastern Mediterranean liqueurs of these ingredients

SAMBUCO

Water-white Italian liqueur combining the freshness of witch elderbush with liquorice flavour.

TRES CASTILLOS

A Puerto Rican anisette with sugar candy.

KÜMMEL

Caraway seeds are excellent aids to digestion, which we can enjoy in cakes and bread and as the flavour of liqueurs. These properties of caraway have been known for centuries and the plant was profusely cultivated in Holland in the middle ages. Even today we can enjoy caraway flavoured cheeses and rye bread, and in our cradles probably enjoyed the weakly alcoholic caraway flavoured liquid called Gripe Water.

The earliest recorded European caraway liqueur was made by Lucas Bols in his small Amsterdam distillery in 1575—*Bolskümmel* is still famous today.

The movement of *kümmel* distillation from West to East Europe is referred to the visit of Peter the Great of Russia, who visited Amsterdam in 1696. Being anxious to establish a Russian Navy, he decided to learn shipbuilding at first hand and worked as a labourer, keeping his identity secret. During his eighteen month stay, he visited the Bols distillery and thus it is believed that he brought *kümmel* to Russia. Production did not, in fact, commence until the early part of the nineteenth century with manufacture at the Allash distillery.

The best known Allash *kümmel* came from the Allash estate of Mentzendorff, in Labura. After the first world war, the manufacture ceased in Labura after the Mentzendorff family left, and the London agent—Blankenhagen—arranged manufacture of Mentzendorff *kümmel* at Stettin, in Germany. This is now the only *kümmel* which may be called Allash.

Famous Riga *kümmels* were made by the Wolfschmidt family, who were represented in England from the middle of the nineteenth century by Maurice Meyer and later by his daughter, the late Mrs. Mary Fisher, who took over his business on his death in 1918. From that time on she devoted herself to the building up of the firm, Maurice Meyer, of which she remained managing director until her retirement in 1961. She died two years later, aged 83.

In her early years in business, she found the position rather strange for in those days such a career for a woman was most unusual. Her ability, industry and perspicacity soon achieved for her a niche which she occupied with distinction for the rest of her life. She had a remarkable palate and her opinion was frequently sought. After she had been in business for some time, she decided to specialise in liqueurs and acquired a great reputation as an expert in this branch of the trade. Before the last war she listed nearly 200 liqueurs, most of them from Europe, and some from other parts of the world. Her knowledge was fully recognised by her friends in the trade, and she frequently lectured on liqueurs.

She was the author of the first book on the subject of liqueurs and often contributed to various magazines and newspapers, and also broadcast.

At the time of her death she was engaged on her auto-biography, 'Recollections of a Woman Wine Merchant,' which is being edited for future publication.

Wolfschmidt made several types of *kümmel*, which were all available in the U.K. until the second world war.

ALLASH TYPE—typical *kümmel* liqueur (sold at 72° proof).

JAGD KÜMMEL—hunting *kümmel* sold in stone jars with highly colourful labels depicting hunting scenes (sold at 87° proof).

Dry unsweetened *kümmel* (sold at 86° proof).

Crystallised *kümmel* OO (sold at 97° proof).

CRÈME DE CUMIN—the finest of all *kümmel* was sold 103° proof in thin crystal bottles with a large pointed punt on which were formed sugar crystals giving the appearance of a snow covered mountain. *Cumin* is a dwarf plant of Egyptian origin related to the caraway family and cultivated throughout Southern Europe. Another famous pre-war *kümmel* was the *Eckau OO* of Count Pahlen.

The finest *kümmels* of today are made in Holland, including the Wolfschmidt brand. This is a consequence of the disappearance of Latvia. Other recognised brands are Mentzendorff, Fockink and Bols, but of course, most distillers produce a *kümmel*.

GILKA KÜMMEL

Is drier than Allash and the best known of the type classified as Berliner *kümmel*, now produced in Hamburg. *Gilka* quality has been acknowledged for over 130 years.

C.L.O.C. (CUMIN LIQUIDUM OPTIMUM CASTELLI)

A fine Danish caraway liqueur literally ' The best caraway in the castle.' It is water-white and at 55° proof, weaker than Dutch *kümmel*.

DANZIG GOLDWASSER

This has been produced in Danzig by the firm of Der Lachs from 1598 and today's bottle is still embossed with the picture of a salmon (der Lachs).

The original liqueur was water-white, flavoured with aniseed and caraway, the gold flakes only being added when it became known that gold was valuable in the treatment of certain diseases. In India, in the Palaces of great Princes, gold dust used to be sprinkled on sweet courses at important functions, to honour the guest and to aid digestion, and it is not surprising that considerable quantities of Der Lachs were sold to India before the war.

After wartime destruction of the Der Lachs, Danzig establishment, the liqueur is now produced in West Berlin to the original Danzig formula.

DANZIG SILBERWASSER

Identical to *Danzig Goldwasser* with silver leaves instead of gold flakes. Although the flavour is identical, this version appears far less palatable with silver than with gold!

LIQUEUR D'OR

Most French and Dutch manufacturers now produce Goldwater, Garnier in France being the first in 1890.

MINT LIQUEURS

The digestive properties of the various types of mint have long been known, and the most used variety in liqueurs, *labiatae*, belongs to the same sweet herb family as garden mint.

Every liqueur producer manufactures *crème de menthe*, a mint or peppermint flavoured spirit sweetened and sold white or coloured green. Mitcham, in Surrey, was supposed to grow the finest mint and continental distillers imported it from there. The best known green variety is ' *Freezomint*,' made by Cusenier, who have been making liqueurs for over 100 years, starting from the family home in the Jura mountains. They eventually moved to Paris. Eighty years ago they built a second distillery in Marseilles and today their products are world renowned.

A second popular brand is *Pippermint*, of Get Frères, in its own uniquely shaped bottle, available green and white.

MENTUCCIA

' Little piece of mint ' is also known as *Centerbe*, because it is said to be compounded from 100 herbs gathered at the foot of the Abruzzi mountains, which produce a potent fine flavoured digestive. It is sometimes known after its inventor, Fra. San Silvestro.

Chapter 15

BEAN AND KERNEL LIQUEURS

CRÈME DE CACAO, or Chocolate liqueur, is produced by all manufacturers making the full range of liqueurs, either by maceration or percolation of cacao beans followed by distillation and sweetening. It used to be very popular in the Far East, where it was drunk through a thick layer of cream floating on its surface. It is still extremely popular in the Marseilles area, and for restaurateurs it is most useful for serving with desserts and ice cream sweets.

Crème de Cacao is available colourless or brown, the latter often including a little vanilla and stating on the label ' *Crème de Cacao à la vanille.*'

Several *Crèmes de Cacao* have the additional title Chouao. In the late nineteenth century, the finest cacao beans were grown in a valley near Caracas, in the Chouao valley, which was some dozen miles long and surrounded by forest covered mountains. The colony was founded by monks; the wood from the forest was used to make fine furniture. Now Chouao is a suburb of Caracas, and although the term Chouao is still used on labels, this is now the generic term for Venezuelan cacao beans, as no more beans come from the original Chouao valley.

CACAO MIT NUSS, an interesting white German liqueur, chocolate with hazel nut flavour.

ROYAL MINT-CHOCOLATE

This is a new liqueur which reproduces the exquisite and delicate flavour of the after-dinner mint.

H. Warner Allen wrote in *Liqueurs and the Wine Lover*, " To my amazement and delight when I tried it with my coffee my tongue and palate registered nothing but approval. The coarseness of chocolate had been extracted and the delicate flavour of the cacao berry, which I had not tasted for so many years that I had forgotten it, had been retained. This pleasant, smooth liqueur set me wondering how two tastes to which I thought I was allergic could have been so miraculously adapted to please my palate and came to the conclusion that it was a case of art returning to nature."

Royal Mint-Chocolate Liqueur took about two years to develop. During the course of compounding, I found that making liqueurs is an art rather than a science, and that the invention of a new liqueur could best be paralleled with a composer working on an orchestral composition. The composer knows the sound he is hearing in his mind, and he is then able to pull it apart, giving each member of the orchestra a certain part to play. Similarly, with a liqueur, the final result is visualised; this is theoretically taken apart and then actually put together component by component to give the end-product. The compounding of a liqueur, of course, presents particular difficulties as the ' players ' (special extracts, distillates, etc.), very often inter-act giving very different results, and what is not generally realised is that the sequence of events is of extreme importance. As so often happens, it was pure chance that led to the final result in this case; a dozen independent unsuccessful trials had been mixed at the end of an evening and set aside for kitchen use in preparation of sweets and sorbets. When after a week, by chance, the mixture was tasted, the research was at an end! The answer had been found.

Extensive calculations were then necessary to break down the numerous components into exact quantities, and shortly after, with minor adjustments, ' *Royal Mint-Chocolate* ' *Liqueur* was born. It is now produced and bottled in France. *VANDERMINT* is a Dutch chocolate and mint liqueur presented in a Delft bottle.

COFFEE LIQUEURS

Crème de Café, Crème de Mokka are made in all liqueur producing countries. The liqueurs are usually sweetened spirit extracts of coffee, coloured brown.

Several have become extremely well known.

TIA MARIA is a Jamaican liqueur rum based on Blue Mountain coffee extracts and local spices. The present liqueur was developed by Dr. Kenneth Evans from an age-old recipe whose composition is a closely guarded secret.

KAHLÚA. Mexican coffee liqueur which, for European markets, is made under licence by Heering in Denmark. The liqueur is quite different in style from *Tia Maria* and is very popular in U.S.A.

GALLWEYS IRISH COFFEE LIQUEUR is a smooth, dark brown with a rich coffee flavour. It is whiskey based and partly uses old honey and herb recipes to blend with fragrant coffee.

Also well known are *EXPRESSO* (Italy), *ALOHA* (Scotland) and *PASHA* (Turkey). There are several mokka and coffee liqueurs from Austria and Germany.

CRÈME DE CAFÉ—' Coffee Sport '—A light fresh American coffee liqueur made by Jacquin and presented in a heat resistant coffee pot which can be re-used for real coffee.

COFFEE HOUSE LIQUEUR. A rich liqueur with the robust flavour of Virgin Islands spirit blended with local coffee extracts.

BAHIA. Brazilian coffee blended with local grain spirit with a slightly bitter-sweet tang. Sold in a specially shaped bottle.

MOKKA MIT SAHNE. German coffee liqueur with cream (which must have a 10% fat content).

KIRSCH MIT MOKKA. Coffee and cherry flavoured liqueur made from coffee extracts, cherry juice, plus Kirsch (and Framboise).

NOYAU is a strong sweet liqueur, almond in flavour, which is made from extracts of peach and apricot kernels. There are several producers who offer the liqueur water-white or pink. The finest is the French of Vve. Champion, which has been shipped to Maurice Meyer Ltd., in London, for over eighty years. The company still has Bills of Lading showing shipments of several products from Vve. Champion dated 1869 and 1872.

It is recorded that the original M. Champion came from Martinique and established a distillery in Bordeaux. After his death, over 130 years ago, his widow made over the business to two of her workers, Droz and Jourde, and eventually Alexander Droz became the sole proprietor. His grandson still continues manufacture of Vve. Champion *Noyau*.

KOLA LIQUEURS are made from Kolanuts, citrus peel flavours, tonkabeans and vanilla. Spices may also be added.

CRÈME DE VANILLE. Smooth, rich liqueur made from vanilla beans.

COCONUT WHISQUEUR. A Scotch whisky based coconut liqueur produced for manufacture of liqueur chocolates.

RECENT INTRODUCTIONS

ROYAL ORANGE-CHOCOLATE LIQUEUR (1969). The combination of chocolate and orange has produced a connoisseurs drink. Soft and satisfying on the palate it is best served cool.

ROYAL GINGER-CHOCOLATE LIQUEUR see page 61.

ROYAL CHERRY-CHOCOLATE LIQUEUR (1970) is a fascinating new sensation rich in flavour and very smooth on the palate.

ROYAL BANANA-CHOCOLATE LIQUEUR (1971) is a remarkably interesting combination which was specially produced as a new base for rum cocktails but is delicious served neat.

Chapter 16

FLOWER, BLOSSOM AND LEAF LIQUEURS

JAPANESE GREEN TEA LIQUEUR

A UNIQUELY oriental liqueur. It is made from two fine teas—Matcha, powdered tea, and Gyokuro—rolled tea, which have been grown in Japan for centuries. The combination with grape brandy gives a delightful liqueur, with a subtle perfume of fine tea. Presentation is usually in ceramic bottles. Another tea liqueur is OCHA.

Not many European producers market a *crème de thé* any longer, although I recall tasting ' *Tea Breeze* ' by Marie Brizard, a medium dry, brown liqueur with a taste of spiced tea.

CHERRY BLOSSOM LIQUEUR

Unique to the Japanese house of Suntory Ltd., who are also large producers of malt whiskey. The delicate pink liqueur is said to capture the very essence of fragrant and precious cherry blossoms and mirrors its mysterious bouquet.

CRÈME DE ROSES

Fine delicate French rosé liqueur produced from the essential oils extracted from rose petals. Small quantities of vanilla and citrus oils are normally added. *Gul* is a Turkish brand.

CRÈME DE VIOLETTES

A sweet liqueur made from the petals of violets. *Crème Yvette*, the best known, is the property of Jacquin, in Philadelphia. It was named in honour of the famous French actress, Yvette Gilbert, at the turn of the century.

Chapter 17

MISCELLANEOUS LIQUEURS

ADVOCAAT

A thick creamy liqueur made from the yolks of newlaid eggs and grape brandy. It is the lowest strength 'liqueur' available (approx. 30° proof). Because of its low strength, in the past it had its own Customs descriptive category. Many recipes include small quantities of kirsch, vanilla and citrus peel extracts to enhance the flavour.

Best known are the Dutch advocaats of Bols, Oud, Warnink, de Kuyper ' *Black Hen*,' the Channel Isles *Guernsey Cream* and Seagers *Egg Nog*, which is based on Australian fortified wine. It is particularly popular in mixed drinks with sparkling lemonade (*Snowball*), or with *cherry brandy*.

I have recently tasted an excellent German lemon-flavoured advocaat, but was not impressed with a mokka-flavoured advocaat, although this and chocolate-flavoured advocaat appear to be popular in Germany.

ATHOLL BROSE

Not, strictly speaking, a liqueur but a Scottish drink whose origins go back two centuries. It is composed of Highland malt whisky, uncooked oatmeal made into a brose, honey, cream and secret ingredients to give the special flavour.

BAERENFANG
German honey liqueur based on neutral spirit with extra flavouring from lime flowers and mullein flowers. A Polish honey liqueur is called *KRUPNICK*.

CRÈME DE NOISETTES—nut liqueurs, usually sweet.

CRÈME D'AMANDES—almond liqueurs, usually sweet.

OKHOTNICHYA (HUNTERS BRANDY)
High strength (77° proof) Russian brandy made by infusion of numerous materials, including citrus peel, ginger, galingale, clove, peppers, juniper, coffee and aniseed.

REISHU
Japanese melon liqueur.

PONCHE SOTO
A very popular full brown Spanish liqueur, with a pleasing reminiscence of fine old Sherry. It is presented in a silvered bottle decorated with a silken tassel.

TRYAYOS DEVINERIOS
An old Lithuanian brandy famous for its medicinal properties.

Chapter 18

BRANDY

BRANDY is the spirit distilled from fermented fruit juice (fruit wine) and is the anglicised form of the Dutch *Brantjwyn*, the German *Branntwein* and *Weinbrand*, meaning ' burnt wine.' The French call it *Eau-de-vie-de-vin*.

The generic term brandy as used in England is taken to mean grape brandy—the product obtained by the distillation of grape wine. Some wines, of course, are better suited for distillation than others—the best, from a small, strictly limited area in south-west France are entitled to the name of *Cognac*. The area is sub-divided into seven areas: Grande Champagne, Petite Champagne, Borderies, Fins Bois, Bons Bois, Bois Ordinaires and Bois Communs.

Cognac, which lies some sixty miles north of Bordeaux, is surrounded by vineyards owned by numerous small-holders who produce a rather bitter wine from their vine produce. The quality varies from region to region due to differences in the soil characteristics. Two types of vine are grown—the Folle Blanche and the Colombar. The new wine is distilled in the January and following months of the new year following the vintage, using pot-stills, and it is naturally the distiller who determines the quality of the cognac—

control of the rate of distillation is most important in preserving fine flavours.

The special terms permitted in the marketing of cognacs are:

> COGNAC. This term can only be used if the brandy has been distilled from wines of grapes grown in the Cognac delimited area.

> GRANDE FINE CHAMPAGNE is cognac made from wines of grapes grown only in the Grande Champagne area.

> PETITE CHAMPAGNE is cognac made from wines of grapes grown only in the Petite Champagne area.

> FINE CHAMPAGNE. A cognac made from wines of grapes grown in the Grande and Petite Champagne areas of Cognac, containing at least 50% of the former.

All cognacs must be matured in wooden casks, and oak from the forest of Limoges has been found most suitable. The mellowness and character of a bottled cognac will depend not only on the blender's skill in marrying many casks of different cognacs, but also the length of storage time in cask. Cognac may be coloured slightly with caramel prior to bottling. Once bottled, the spirit will not mature.

Cognacs are marketed either by the name of the French shipper or of the importer. Vintage declarations are usually not stated but are allowed; for cognacs bottled in France the Authorities in Cognac control authenticity; for cognac shipped in cask the importer is responsible for substantiating its age. In the U.K., the landing date of cognac in cask may

8. *Cognac Distillery—Jas. Hennessy & Co.*

9. *Stillroom, Bols Distillery, Schiedam.*

11. Stills, Mampe Distillery, Berlin.

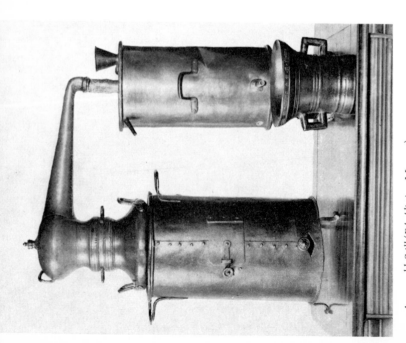

10. A very old Still (Bénédictine Museum).

be stated if it is stored and bottled in bond ' Landed January 1947, bottled March 1967,' a statement which can be checked from Customs and Excise records.

Terms applied to cognacs are:

V.S.O.	Very superior old.
V.S.O.P.	Very superior old pale.
V.V.S.O.P.	Very, very superior old pale.
X.O.	Extremely old.

Grape brandies are made in all wine-producing countries, and those from France, Italy, Greece, Cyprus, Spain, Australia, Israel, U.S.A. (some of which is produced in continuous stills giving spirit of more uniform quality than that produced by pot-still distillation) and the Iron-Curtain countries, are well known and are naturally used in liqueur production. German brandy is not usually distilled from German wine but from other European wines which are less expensive.

PISCO is Peruvian brandy distilled from muscat wines. Similar products are made in other South American countries.

EAU-DE-VIE DE MARCS

Brandy distilled from the fermented pulpy residues after the pressing of grapes for wine is made in most French wine districts. It is called Grappa in Italy and Tresterschnapps in Germany. Many years' maturing are required to smooth the fiery flavour. Recommended method of drinking is to dip a sugar cube into the marc and suck the spirit out! It is often named after the district of origin; thus ' Marc de Bourgogne ' is made from residues of Burgundy pressings. However, brandy distilled from wine lees or wine (e.g. in Burgundy), can be called ' Fine de Bourgogne '—which is usually a less inflammatory product.

ESPRIT DE COGNAC

This is never found as such since it can only be used to 'liqueur' a sparkling wine or champagne. It is produced by a third distillation of cognac and is, by law, high strength.

Chapter 19

GIN

THE production of spirit flavoured with juniper berries has been known for 400 years, and originated in Holland. It is said that a Dutch apothecary, Sylvius of Leyden, first experimented with juniper berries in wine, and then turned to spirits, calling his product *genièvre*—*gin* to us, *geneva* or *genever* to Continentals. It was originally produced for purely medicinal reasons, the juniper being of diuretic value in flushing the urinary system, and the alcohol, of course, acting as a mild stimulant.

Gin has been a popular drink for centuries, and until the mid-eighteenth century, when two Acts of Parliament introduced a licence and control system, production and sale was totally disorganized; *gin* was sold openly in markets and the famous notice, " Drunk for 1d., dead drunk for 2d. " is a reminder of those times. The popularity of *gin* has continued, although the increasing sales of *vodka*, with its freedom of taste, has had an effect. You can still hear of it as Mother's ruin—perhaps a reference to the myth that juniper berries act as an abortifacient.

Gin is produced from neutral grain spirit with the addition not only of juniper, but of other congeners, such as coriander, angelica, caraway, aniseed, orange peel, cardamom, orris root, liquorice root and dozens more, each distiller having his own secret formula not only of mixture proportions, but also of the exact origin of the herbs and spices.

The neutral spirit is usually distilled a second time after reduction in strength to 60 per cent. alcohol. It is, of course, essential for the spirit to be clean and tasteless, and most gin spirit is produced in patent stills from grain. Spirit from other sources such as potatoes is used in some European countries to make *vodka*.

The botanicals are either added to the spirit, which is then distilled and a definite fraction of distillate collected, or vapour extraction methods are used. This is through a ' gin head,' where spirit vapour passes through a layer of botanicals, extracting flavouring en route and selected fractions of distillate again being separated.

Gin is not usually matured before marketing and does not carry any age certificate. The difference in taste between gins is a combination of factors—the distillation technique, the mixture of botanicals and the quality of the spirit.

FLAVOURED GINS

Most flavoured *gins* are produced by steeping the selected fruit in *gin*, although artificial or extracted flavour compounds can be used, but are, of course, second best. Orange and lemon *gins* are still produced, mainly for export markets. Dutch distillers also produce *flavoured gins; blackcurrant gin* is currently available in the U.K.

LONDON GIN

Originally this was *dry gin* produced in or near London, but nowadays there is no geographical significance to the term London. Most modern British and American *gins* are dry and very similar.

PLYMOUTH GIN

Plymouth gin is a heavier, more strongly flavoured gin than the London dry type. It is the popular Royal Navy drink; *pink gin* is made from *Plymouth gin* and angostura bitters.

DUTCH GIN (HOLLANDS, GENEVER or SCHIEDAM)

All Dutch distilleries produce *Holland's gin*, which has a fuller and riper flavour than British or American *gins*. Although the same botanicals are used (in different proportions, of course), it is the nature of the spirit which gives the taste variation and particular character. The spirit is not completely tasteless neutral grain, but spirit which has been distilled in a pot-still from a mash which contains a large proportion of malt, and therefore on distillation, produces some congeners normally associated with whisky. The ' beer ' produced from the cereal mash fermentation is distilled in a pot-still and redistilled at least once, with distillate collected at less than 60 per cent. alcohol. Some *genevers* were quadruple distilled. Finally, the spirit is redistilled with a mixture of botanicals (mainly juniper berries), which gives it a characteristic flavour. This genever is called *Jong*. A second type, *Oud*, is *Jong* genever compounded with distilled grape products, possibly other flavours and may be slightly coloured. It is said that the term ' Dutch Courage ' originated with English soldiers fighting in Europe, who fortified themselves with this very warming drink.

Similarly German manufactured *gin* is *wacholder*.

STEINHAEGER (GERMAN GIN)

It is produced in Westphalia and is colourless, with a distinct juniper flavour and is usually marketed in stone flagons.

Production is by distillation of fermented juniper berries, and the product may be diluted with water and pure spirit only. Juniper berries may be added to increase the flavour, but other additional flavours are not permitted.

The minimum strength is 66.5° proof. Similar production methods are used for:

Borovicka (Slovakia).

Kranawitter (Tirol).

Klekowatsch (Balkans).

OLD TOM GIN

A slightly sweetened (2—6 per cent.) *London gin*, hardly seen in the U.K., but still popular in export markets, particularly in cold climates. The name is credited to a Captain Bradstreet, who is said to have nailed the sign of a cat to his London house, and with a tube served *gin* through the cat's paw! Payment was through the cat's mouth.

The original gin sling was ' *Tom Collins*,' made from *Old Tom gin*, while ' *John Collins* ' was made with *London gin*.

GOLDEN COCK GIN

Norwegian *gin* reputedly one of the smoothest produced.

PEPPERMINT SCHNAPPS

Dry, white peppermint flavoured pot-still spirit of the *aquavit/steinhaeger/genever* type frequently used in dry cocktails to replace *crème de menthe*. It is made in Germany and U.S.A.

PIMMS No. 1, GIN SLING

A flavoured gin based speciality drink designed to be served as a long drink by dilution with sparkling lemonade, garnished with fruit slices, cucumber, mint and borage.

[Pimms Nos. 2-6 were based respectively on whisky, brandy, rum, rye whiskey, vodka, but they have now been withdrawn from the market.]

Chapter 20

VODKA

VODKA is an original Eastern European beverage, and although it is thought of as the Russian national drink, it is believed by some authorities to have a Polish background.

European *vodka* is spirit obtained from potato (although grain spirit is now used in reproducing old *vodka* types) and is, after a second pot-still distillation, filtered through charcoal which removes all flavour and bouquet characteristics. The spirit, which has a remarkable smoothness, is not normally aged although some *vodka* produced in Holland is matured for at least five years in wood.

As with all spirits, the quality is largely dependent upon the nature of the base spirit and the water used in diluting the high strength spirit. With flavoured *vodkas*, of course, wood maturing adds smoothness of flavour.

Vodka or *wodka* means ' little water ' and appears to have been known for eight centuries. The records mention that Russian *vodka* was first distilled in the twelfth century mainly for medicinal purposes. Distilleries appeared in neighbouring countries, and *vodka* became popular especially in the cold Northern countries. It is, of course, regrettably impossible to trace the exact origins.

The *vodkas* produced in Great Britain and the U.S.A. are fairly tasteless, neutral, highly rectified grain spirit whose main virtue is that in mixed drinks the spirit can be ' felt but not smelt,' a far cry from the original Eastern European *vodkas* with characteristic flavour, which are enjoyable on their own.

Russian *vodka* is said to be the *Petrovskaya* type based on a seventeenth century formula invented by Peter the Great. All spirit production is now in the hands of the Russian State Monopoly, Prodintorg.

The fashion for *vodka mixes* came out of California, and has gradually spread eastward, back from whence *vodka* originated. Statistics show that *vodka* (British and American types) sales are steadily increasing and will continue to do so for the spirit ' that leaves you breathless.'

Vodka was introduced to England about seventy years ago, when Maurice Meyer imported *Riga Wodka* from the House of Wolfschmidt. Before the war, when supplies from Latvia ceased, the Riga formula was reproduced in Holland and sold under the brand of ' *Nicholoff* ' after long maturing in cask. In the last decade, *vodka* has become one of the most widely marketed spirits, much of its popularity coming from its lack of taste, which makes it very suitable for mixed drinks. It is, of course, a superb drink with smoked fish when it is drunk neat. Many hors d'oeuvres dishes prove unsuitable for wine drinking, but the perfect accompaniment is provided by *vodka*, especially the Dutch, the Polish *Vyborowa* or *Wyborowa* types and Russian *Stolichnaya* types.

High strength *vodkas* are imported from Russia (*Krepkaya*, 98° proof), and Poland (140° white spirit neutral *vodka*); the Western brand leader, *Smirnoff*, is also available at high strength (80° proof).

SUBROWKA (ZUBROWKA)

Polish *vodka* flavoured by steeping Zubrowka grass (bison grass), resulting in a spirit with a delicate aromatic bouquet. The specially shaped bottle usually contains a stem of the grass. Because of the colour from the grass, it is sometimes known as *green vodka*.

STARKA

Old Russian *vodka* prepared from an infusion of leaves of Crimean apple and pear varieties, plus a dash of *brandy* and *port-type*. The *vodka* is mellow with a pleasing bouquet with a hint of wine flavour.

Polish *Starka* is high strength *vodka* aged in wood; *Krakus* is a specially fine quality vodka; *Winiak* is golden brown 75° proof Polish vodka matured in wine casks for five years.

YUBILEYNAYA OSOBAYA (Jubilee Vodka)

A vodka introduced in 1957 containing cognac, honey and other ingredients.

PERTSOVKA (Pepper Vodka)

A dark brown Russian pepper *vodka* with a pleasing aroma and burning taste, it is said to be good in treating stomach disorders. It is prepared from an infusion of capsicum, cayenne and cubeb.

NICHOLOFF RED VODKA

A vodka of exquisite taste and shimmering colour made from an old Southern Russian recipe. It was reconstructed in

1963 by Pat Simon based on five-year old Dutch vodka, which gives it luxurious smoothness. It is an excellent base for mixed drinks with Vermouth, with tonic and with tomato juice.

Dry
Rowanberry

Allash
Kummel

Subrowka

Monopol

Gothic

Smirnow

Shapes of bottles, pre-war Riça Rowanberry, Kümmel and Wodkas
(Maurice Meyer Ltd. 1934 List).

Chapter 21

AQUAVIT AND OTHER SPIRITS

AQUAVIT, AKVAVIT (Scandinavian Spirit)

SMØRGÅSBORD, or Smørrebrød, and *Aquavit* are ideal partners—the wonderful cold buffet and the cool, clear perfumed spirit of Scandinavia. *Aquavit* is certainly the national drink of Denmark, Sweden, Norway and Iceland and is made either from potato or grain spirit flavoured mainly with caraway, but also with citrus peel and herbs. Swedish *aquavit* has been sold by licence for almost five centuries; some of it is made from potato spirit, which is rectified and charcoal filtered.

The Danish *aquavit* is generally considered the finest, and all Scandinavian spirits are produced under strictest Government control; in Norway, Sweden and Iceland by the Government monopoly.

' *Tafelaquavit* ' is very fine *aquavit*, where the spirit for distillation contains *kümmel*, whose flavour is distilled into the final product.

The best known brands are the Danish *Aarlborg* (which has been distilled in Aarlborg since 1846), Swedish *O. P. Anderson* and Norwegian *Gamel* and *Linie*. The latter is a speciality spirit which is carried across the ' line ' (Equator) by Wilhelmsen liners on return voyages to Australia. The pale yellow colour comes from long maturing in American oak casks.

KORNBRANNTWEIN

German spirit made exclusively from Kornsprit (neutral spirit from mashed corn). The spirit may be flavoured, e.g. *Wachholderkornbrannt*—juniper flavoured.

DOPPELKORN

As above, but at least 38% alcohol (66.5° proof).

SNAPS, SCHNAPPS

Strong dry Dutch and German spirits which may be flavoured. In Scandinavia, the terms are generic to include *aquavit*.

TEQUILA (Mexican Spirit)

Mexico, the land of the cactus, makes use of this plant in the manufacture of *tequila*. The agave cactus (also known as the century plant, or mezcal) may take a decade to reach maturity, and when it does, its heart (pineapple shaped and full of sap) is removed and the juice extracted.

Fermentation of the juice is followed by distillation in a pot-still. It is frequently bottled at high strength and not often aged in wood, and may have been twice distilled. *Tequila* is harsh and is consumed in Mexico with salt and fresh lime juice—the juice is squeezed onto the tongue, followed by a small amount of salt, and only then—the *tequila*. Only the spirit distilled in or near the town of *Tequila* is entitled to be called *tequila*. From other regions the spirit is called *mezcal*.

OKELEHAO (Hawaiian Spirit)

' Oke ' is produced by distillation in a column still of the fermented mash of Ti plant roots. The distillate may be charcoal filtered before bottling. It is said to have an interesting and unusual flavour.

NG KA PY

Taiwan Formosan liqueur.

MUI KWE LU, MOW TOY WINE

75° and 90° proof high-strength spirits made from Kaoliang grain spirit, shipped to the U.K. from Hong Kong.

ARRAK (East Indies Spirit)

The most famous is Indonesian, Batavia Arrak from the Island of Java, best described as a brandy-like rum. The spirit is produced as a rum from molasses fermented with natural yeasts, including specially cooked rice in the mixture. (Some Eastern manufacture includes coconut juice, or the juice of palm trees is used, in which case the distilled product is called toddy.) It is said that the combination of river water and natural yeast activity gives a special flavour which is very popular in Sweden, where the Batavia Arrak is sweetened, flavoured and compounded into a liqueur called Arrack Punsch or Caloric Punsch.

Batavia Arrak is usually wood matured for several years. It is dry and highly pungent.

Most Eastern countries produce ' arrak ' types, mainly from rice and sugar, but often including local fermentable produce. Many Mediterranean countries produce similar spirits which carry the generic title ' arrak ' but bear little resemblance to the original Batavia Arrak; they may be flavoured with local spices and are usually harsh and immature products.

TIQUIRA

High strength Brazilian spirit obtained by distillation of malted and fermented tapioca roots.

SAKÉ

Japanese rice wine, which is not a liqueur although it is brewed to 30° proof by simultaneous processes which convert starch to sugar and then to alcohol. The ferments are Koji and Saké yeast. The distilled spirit is also recorded as *Saké*.

SHOCHU

Japanese colourless spirit obtained by distillation of the fermentation products of sweet potatoes.

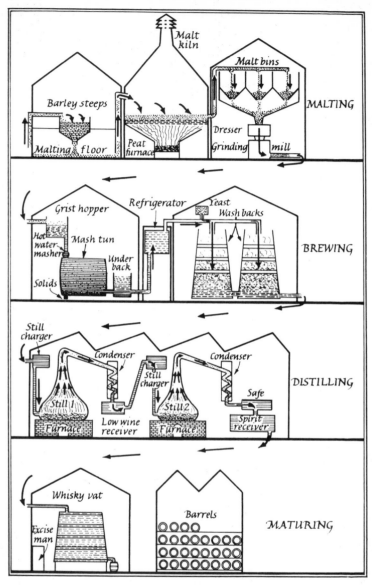

MALTING

Malt kiln

Barley steeps

Malting floor · Peat furnace

Malt bins

Dresser · Grinding mill

BREWING

Grist hopper · Refrigerator · Yeast · Wash backs

Hot water masher · Mash tun

Under back

Solids

DISTILLING

Still charger · Condenser · Condenser

Still charger · Safe

Still 1 · Low wine receiver · Still 2 · Spirit receiver

Furnace · Furnace

MATURING

Whisky vat · Barrels

Excise man

Diagram of a distillery

12. *The Peat fire—Scotch Malt Whisky production.*

13. *Pot-stills—Scotch Malt Whisky production.*

14. Gin Distillery, James Burrough Ltd., London. Rectifying stills on the left; pot-stills on the right.

Chapter 22

WHISKY

THE term *whisky* is undoubtedly of Celtic origin, derived from the Gaelic (the branch of Celtic spoken in the highlands)—'uisge beatha' or 'usqua'—which means 'water of life.'

It is, of course, impossible to locate the true origins of whisky-making, whether it was brought to Scotland by monks or whether it originated in Ireland. The sites of some of the finest distilling centres of today—Speyside, Islay and Kintyre, were once the sites of monastic communities.

Although modern methods have been introduced into the distilleries, the old methods are retained as much as possible to keep the style and character. All pot-stills are made of copper—a most useful material with good thermal conductivity, high resistance to corrosion and an ability to be worked into the complex shapes of the still. Several distilleries market their products individually, but the general trend is for blended whiskies which are saleable much younger than single unblended malt whisky.

Two types of whisky are produced in Scotland, *malt whisky* and *grain whisky*. The former, a pot-still spirit, is heavy and very flavoury, whereas the latter is light and because it is distilled at a higher temperature, has less flavour

H

than malt whisky. A blend of malt and grain whiskies produces a desirable balance and to satisfy many tastes in different world markets, the blender will arrange his component malts and grains in different proportions, possibly selecting a fuller flavoured blend for cold countries. Colour, of course, is no indication of flavour—many fine-blended whiskies are bottled at natural light yellow to gold colour without addition of caramel colouring.

It is, of course, interesting and certainly scientifically inexplicable why several distilleries in the same area produce different whiskies, naturally with certain common characteristics, and this remains one of the great mysteries of Scotch.

AMERICAN WHISKEYS

Bourbon, Rye and Wheat Whiskeys are, by definition, whiskey distilled at less than 80% alcohol from a fermented mash of at least 51% corn, rye or wheat respectively. The law, until recently, insisted on new charred oak casks being used for storage but now allow ' used ' casks to be filled, much to the disappointment of distillers in Scotland, who imported them and who may now have difficulty in obtaining casks.

Many American whiskeys are labelled ' Bottled in Bond,' which does not have the same meaning as in the U.K. Obviously, the whiskey is bottled under government supervision, but with the extra stipulation that the strength is not less than 100 U.S. proof, it is four years old, and that it was the product of one distilling season and one producer. The government tax slip which is fixed over the capsule is green for bonded whiskeys, re ' for all other whiskeys.

MOONSHINE

Illicit whiskey; produced in the hills without licence, drunk strong and rough.

CANADIAN WHISKEY

Rye flavoured whiskies distilled in Canada in similar fashion to the best Kentucky bourbons.

OTHER WHISKIES

Popular ones in the Far East are produced in Australia and Japan. Whisky types are also produced in Holland, Germany and Denmark.

AMERICAN WHISKEY TERMS

'SOUR MASH,' a term applied frequently to whiskeys, particularly Bourbon. The name refers to the natural fermentation of yeast and grain, where de-alcoholised ferment from the previous distillation is added to the mash. Continuity of flavour is guaranteed and it can be thought of as a form of 'solera.'

'STRAIGHT WHISKEY'

Pure whiskey (Bourbon, Rye, Corn) to which only pure water is added to reduce to the desired strength. The law states a minimum ageing of two years in wooden charred casks; it may not have been distilled at more than 80% alcohol and may not be sold at less than 40% alcohol.

The whiskey must have been produced from a grain mixture of at least 51% of the grain type with which the whiskey is named.

'BLENDED WHISKEY'

Blends of 'straight whiskey' and neutral spirits.

BRANCH WATER

Spring water from a small tributary stream said to be the only suitable dilutant for the finest whiskies.

GRAIN WHISKEY

Scotch, Irish and American whiskeys. The selected grain (mostly imported maize for Scotch whisky production) is pulverised and warmed with malted barley (p. 101) and water, the enzyme activity changing the starches into sugar (dextrose). Addition of yeast starts the fermentation of this 'wort' which takes several days.

Alcohol, carbon dioxide and other products are thus formed; this mixture (wash) is heated and the alcoholic vapours distilled off—the middle fractions are collected and matured in wooden casks. In Scotland, after three years maturing the spirit may be called whisky.

The patent stills used for grain whiskies are of the continuous coffey type. The still consists of two very large vertical columns placed consecutively, one the analyser, the second the rectifier. Each column consists of a series of perforated plates. The cold wash enters at one end and meets steam introduced under pressure from the other end. This distils the alcohol which, in turn, is condensed by the cold new wash, which itself is warmed in the process of heat exchange. The distillation is continuous and although the plant is called the 'Coffey' still, the method was, in fact, invented by Robert Stein, an Irish distiller who patented the process in 1826.

MALT WHISKY

Scotch malt whisky is made from barley, much of which is locally grown, but a great amount imported. Quality control is most important and each distillery makes certain that only best quality barley goes into the malting stage and inferior quality is rejected.

Production of malt whisky can be broken down in well-defined separate stages—malting, mashing, fermenting, distilling and finally maturing.

MALTING

After elimination of inferior grain, the barley is softened by thorough soaking in water for two to three days. It is then spread over the stone floor of the malting house, where it is kept warm and moist, and the barley germinates. In due course, the grain sprouts and in the process the starch has been changed into maltose by enzymic action of diastase.

Germination usually takes seven to ten days, but may take three weeks, and should be a steady process. The roots which form may interweave, and in order to stop this and aerate the grain the·'floor' is turned at least twice daily, carefully to avoid any damage. The grain must be kept moist and temperature control is important.

The sprouting grain is now heated in a kiln over a peat fire, which stops germination and dries the grain for milling. It is, of course, the peat smoke which gives a characteristic flavour which remains right through the following processes, and is, of course, the unmistakeable flavour of Scotch. The flavour of the whisky is much dependent upon the kilning process.

MASHING

The kilned malt is ground into 'grist,' thoroughly mixed with warm water, and the soluble starch is completely converted into sugars (mainly maltose) by the action of the diastase. The residual husks are removed for use as cattle feed. The mixture known as 'wort' is now fermented by the addition of yeast, and then contains alcohol and other products, including by-products of the fermentation and coincident bacterial action. The fermentation takes about two days to complete.

This weakly alcoholic solution 'wash' (approximately 10%), is pumped into the wash still where distillation produces a distillate, which is also weakly alcoholic—'low wines' (approximately 20% alcohol).

'Low wines' are redistilled in a different still, and only the middle fraction is useful spirit—Scotch malt whisky at approximately 70% alcohol. The first part of the distillation 'heads' and the end part of the distillation 'tails' are known as 'feints' and these are added to the next batch of low wines, their useful contents thus being preserved. These fractions usually contain high proportion of acids, fusel oils and aldehyde contaminants.

Distillers can control, within limits, the flavour of the distillate, and it has been said that mild peat flavour is best produced by slow distillation, whereas heavy peat flavour is obtained by rapid distillation over hotter fires. The heating of the 'wash' during the first distillation causes changes in minor constituents, which are vital to the flavour and character of the whisky.

The useful spirit fraction must, of course, be reduced in strength for maturing and 111° proof is accepted by most distillers. It is most important that pure water is used in reducing the strength of the whisky, and the quality of this water also is important in determining the flavour of the final product.

Four main types of Scotch malt whisky are produced according to their district of distillation.

Highland.—Considered the finest malts, light in flavour, delicate in body and smokiness. The *Glenlivet* and *Speyside* whiskies are considered the best.

Lowland.—Light bodied, flavoury.

Campbeltowns.—Very full bodied smokey malt whiskies.

Islay.—Very full bodied, smoky flavoured, sometimes very strong. Excellent blending whiskies.

Both malt and grain types of whisky distilled in Scotland are legally entitled only to the term ' spirits ' until they have been aged in cask for a minimum of three years, at which time they may be called Scotch whisky. Scotch whisky exported to the U.S.A. must be aged four years in cask.

Maturing in wooden casks is a most important stage in the development of any pot-stilled spirit which contains fusel oils, aldehydes and other intensely flavoured products (congeners), which make the newly distilled spirit sharp in flavour. In cask the whisky is in contact with air and wood, and because of this, physical and chemical changes take place—some compounds oxidise, some interact because of the oxygen of the air, some compounds are absorbed by the wood, and certain compounds and colour are drawn from the wood, and some may interact through a catalytic effect of the tannins or other compounds in the wood. The overall result is that the whisky develops fine bouquet and flavours, becomes slightly coloured and mellows. During the ageing process there is an obvious loss in volume and alcoholic strength through evaporation—the damper the climate, the smaller the loss of volume—the hotter the storage temperature, the higher the loss of volume and strength, accompanied by an increased rate of maturation, though not necessarily a better maturation.

For the finest whiskies, distillers prefer to use recently emptied sherry casks.

Many single distillery malt whiskies are now commercially available usually after lengthy maturing in cask. The finest are sold at eight, ten or twelve years old, and are equal to the finest liqueurs; they are dry of course, without sweetening.

Whisky drinking in the early nineteenth century was fairly restricted due to the unblended malt whiskies not being to everybody's taste. It was not until the latter part of the century that grain whisky, which is practically tasteless and characterless, was used to dilute the heavy malt flavour, and made whisky into an ever increasingly popular drink.

The grain distilleries are mainly built in the Lowlands, and with the natural Lowland-Highland rivalry, in 1905 proceedings commenced to limit the use of the words Scotch whisky to the malts, but the case was not decided. The controversy was finally settled by a Royal Commission in 1909, which decided that Scotch whisky was 'obtained by distillation in Scotland from a mash of cereal grain saccharified by the diastase of malt,' a definition which, of course, includes the production of grain whisky.

The more recent 1952 Customs and Excise Act has the additional requisite 'matured in bonded warehouse in casks for three years.' A noted exception to this regulation is the immature whisky shipped to the Spirit Monopoly in Sweden, who warehouse the spirit for three years before offering it for sale as 'Scotch Whisky.'

IRISH MALT WHISKEY

This usually has a softer smokiness than Scotch, which may be due to the best fraction of distillate being taken at lower strength than Scotch malt during a third distillation and also because the malted grain is dried in a kiln without contact with the peat smoke which is so essential for giving flavour to Scotch Whisky. Known as *Usquebaugh*, it is thought to have first been produced in the thirteenth century.

There are several distilleries in Eire (operating as one company) and one (Bushmills) in Northern Ireland.

POTEEN or POCHEEN

The name for illicitly distilled Irish Whiskey—labels not to be found!

Chapter 23

RUM

R^{UM} is a generic term for a series of spirits produced from the fermented juice of sugar cane or molasses. *Rums* are produced in practically all sugar growing countries.

The name *rum* is derived from either of two words used in the West Indies in the seventeenth century—rumbullion and rumbustion—and it is thought that it originated in the East. It is quite definite that rum was produced in the West Indies in the seventeenth century. In those days, the spirit was crude and drunk mainly by slaves—nowadays, with modern methods of production, *rum* has become a sophisticated drink which lends itself to numerous delicious mixed drinks.

Rum production is based on a standard procedure, with variations according to country. Freshly cut sugar cane is crushed to extract the juice which is then concentrated by boiling to a syrup. The sugar in the syrup is crystallised in a high speed centrifuge and the residual molasses are the basis for *rum* manufacture which can be made either as light or heavy *rums*.

The French, however, until 1921 used to distinguish between the following:

EAU-DE-VIE DE CANNE, the spirit obtained by distillation of fermented sugar cane juice (natural or slightly concentrated).

LE RHUM, the spirit obtained by distillation of fermented sugar cane juice to which had been added residues of previous distillation.

LE TAFIA (Créole word), the spirit obtained by distillation of fermented molasses after extraction of the raw sugar.

1. LIGHT RUM—PUERTO RICA, CUBA, S. AMERICA, etc.

The molasses diluted with water and residues from the previous distillation are fermented with cultured yeast, and the resulting low alcoholic liquid distilled in a column still, so as to collect distillate of high strength (80% alcohol), which results in a neutral flavoured light rum, generally low in congeners. The important middle fraction only is matured in wood, and before bottling, it is clarified and filtered through sand and charcoal. If the rum is to be sold dark in colour, caramel must be added, which ensures continuity of type.

2. FULL BODIED RUM (*a*) JAMAICA

The molasses are diluted with water and also with the residues from the sugar boilers and fermented with natural yeasts, assisted by residues from a previous fermentation. The weakly alcoholic solution is distilled in a pot-still and the resulting 'low wine' redistilled when the middle distillate fraction (produced at less than 80% alcohol) is collected and matured in wood. The rum is usually coloured with caramel prior to bottling. The full bodied rum is, of course, richer in congeners (giving a heavy pungent fullness) and requires longer than light rums to reach smoothness.

(*b*) DEMERARA RUM, as Jamaica rum, but distillation is by column still in place of pot-still.

Quality variation between rums is due to natural factors, such as the quality of the sugar cane (character), the climate and the soil factor, as well as the method of distillation.

The characteristic bouquet is in some part due to bacterial action during fermentation, which causes some acetic acid formation.

Rum	Colour	Flavour	Body
Puerto Rico	light	delicate	light
Virgin Islands	light	slight	light
Jamaica	golden	rich—full	full
Demerara	dark	rich	less than Jamaica
Barbados	amber	very strong	medium—may be flavoured
Martinique	dark	pronounced	medium—may be flavoured
New England	amber	full, heavy	Produced in patent stills full—from W. Indian molasses
Batavia arrack (Java)		dry, aromatic	—may include rice in the molasses
Cuba	light	dry	light —may be flavoured
S. America	light	dry	light

Rum is a magnificent base for long mixed drinks, and large numbers have been recorded. The characteristic flavour allows a great proportion of diluting juice (fruit, soda, cola) to be used without losing a flavoursome drink.

Some of the mixtures, known as punch, may have originated in the fortification of lime juice which was preserved for ship's stores use by adding spirit to the juice. British sailors drank lime juice as protection against scurvy and obtained the nickname 'Limeys' from Americans. The British Customs manual still includes regulations for the fortification of lime and lemon juices.

RUM VERSCHNITT

A German blended spirit which contains at least 5% rum, usually highly flavoured high ether rum. '*Echter-Rum*' is 100% imported rum reduced with pure water to marketing strength.

Chapter 24

LIQUEURS IN THE KITCHEN
By Elaine Hallgarten

I AM sure that no self-respecting cook has not, at some time, had harsh words with the master of the house over the amount of spirituous matter finding its way into the kitchen. However, any discerning husband can soon be pacified by the results of his wife's efforts with his liqueurs.

Simple casseroles are enhanced, as we know, by the addition of wine, but brandy, too, is an important partner in many dishes, especially chicken. Other spirits and liqueurs find their way into recipe books for all courses and types of food. Common sense, as well as a good recipe, can often produce wonders. For instance, calvados goes with pheasant, its apple flavour blending with that of the game, and equally this spirit adds its own distinctive touch to chicken, sautéed with fresh herbs. Many recipes for meat dishes call for a dash of brandy and indeed few common-or-garden stews would not be the better for a judicious shot of brandy. Terrines and pâtés often include a brandy or liqueur in their ingredients—not only for its obvious improvement in flavour, but also for helping the keeping properties of the dish.

Undoubtedly it is for desserts that we can find the major outlet for our imaginative powers with liqueurs and brandy.

A good many of the liqueur companies publish their own, often very beautifully produced, leaflets, which are available to the public. An adventurous hostess can find some exciting ideas through these leaflets.

As a general rule, the fruit based liqueurs are the most versatile in dessert cookery. Any basic soufflé recipe can be adapted to include a liqueur—*Grand Marnier* is most often seen on restaurant menus, but *Maraschino*, *Glen Mist*, *Bénédictine*, or almost any liqueur you like, can be substituted. Using a purée of fruit together with *Kirsch* is a variation which might appeal to those who care for this spirit. *Kirsch* added to whipped cream can make even the most mundane fruit salad into a special dessert, but you may prefer to add a small ' dosage ' to the salad itself, in which case, again, any of the fruit based liqueurs are admirable. An unusual way of flavouring a fruit salad is to ' lift ' the taste of selected fruits with liqueurs: slices of apple could be marinaded in *Calvados*, cherries in *Maraschino* or *Kirsch*, pears in *Poire William*, plums in *Quetsch* or *Slivovitz*, apricots in *Brandy*, to make a potent ' fruit cocktail.'

Prunes are usually considered to be ' nursery ' fare, but in France they become a delicacy when steeped in *Armagnac*. Some people consider that they have a better flavour if soaked in weak tea rather than plain water.

After the novelty of having fruit at the beginning of its season has worn a little thin, a quick and delicious change can be wrought by soaking the fruit in liqueur. Strawberries thus treated sometimes carry the name ' Kloobnika Romanoff ' and even the most devoted of strawberry eaters, who will swear there is nothing you can do to a strawberry to improve on its natural taste, will agree that a cold bath of *vodka, rum* and *curaçao* (in equal proportions) turns a bowl of juicy, fresh strawberries into a dessert for which the wildest superlatives are not too much.

Yet another variation on the fruit plus liqueur theme, and again a simple but effective dessert, is the flambéeing of fruit, which restaurants do with such panache. The would-be maître d'hotel can start with the less expensive fruits—bananas (with *rum*) and apples (with *calvados*) and work up to the more exotic peaches (with *brandy*) and pineapples (with *Kirsch*).

While on the subject of flambéeing, I must mention crêpes, which, by common usage, are allied to almost any combination of liqueurs to produce a dramatic finale to a meal. Few people even realise that the dish for which they pay so highly in a smart restaurant, which is invariably called 'Crêpes Suzette,' is a somewhat bastardised version of the original. Most people are happy to accept a soggy pancake, over which has been poured and set alight a mixture of liqueurs—all this done to an accompaniment of commis waiters hurrying to and fro with oranges, lemons, sugar and butter. Legends abound as to the origins of Crêpes Suzette, but on one factor all true cooks agree, and that is the content of these delectable pancakes. Larousse Gastronomique notes that Crêpes Suzette consist of thin pancakes, stuffed with a mixture of butter, sugar, the juice of a mandarin orange and some *curaçao*. There is no mention of drowning the pancake in a variety of liqueurs and, perhaps more surprisingly, not a word about flambé. However, for those non-purists among us, Crêpes Suzette, as generally made, can, if carefully prepared, make a most pleasing dessert.

The liqueurs which come under the heading of 'Herb based' are by no means the Cinderellas of the family *vis-à-vis* cookery. Most can indeed be used in a similar way to the fruit liqueurs, adapting to soufflés and crêpes. The delicate balance of herbs with fruit make many of this group of liqueurs particularly suitable with fruit salads or individual fruits. They also lend themselves well to creamy concoctions, for cake fillings. Madame Prunier suggests a pancake filling using *Chartreuse*, or equally effectively, *Vieille Cure* or *Bénédictine*. A basic mousse recipe can be 'laced' with a Scotch liqueur, such as *Glen Mist*, in which blackberries or other soft fruit may be used. The combinations and permutations are endless and limited only by the ingenuity of the cook.

The bean or kernel type of liqueurs suggest their own uses. What chocolate mousse could not be greatly improved with a touch of coffee liqueur? What 'poires Hélène' could not be raised to the heights of perfection with some *Royal Mint-Chocolate*? Any basically creamy dessert would be suitable for using this category of liqueurs and as a topping for ice creams they are particularly apt since they tend to blend well with the rich, creaminess of the ice. Any type of liqueur can be added in this way, and the fruit liqueurs make natural dessert fellows with sorbet ices.

For those who leave sufficient liqueur in the cellar after trying out a few of these ideas, or for others who at heart prefer to drink their liqueurs, there are numerous varieties of drinks mixing hot coffee with different liqueurs to make exotic sounding beverages. Several restaurant groups make a speciality of their coffee drinks and offer an impressive selection using a full range of liqueurs. This would not be outside the reach of any hostess since these are very simple to make and as most of the liqueurs are available in miniature bottles it would be possible to keep quite a selection, from which guests could choose their own favourite.

The following is a small selection of well tried recipes, as published by the liqueur houses and importers:

CHERRY HEERING CUCUMBER APPETISER

Split a cucumber lengthwise and scoop out the pips. Blend with care some Danish cream cheese and Heering's *Cherry Brandy*. Fill the cucumber halves with this mixture and chill. Cut into slices and serve.

HOMARD FLAMBÉ DU VIEUX MOINE

Cut a lobster in half lengthwise, and lay two halves shell downwards on a metal dish.

Season the flesh, sprinkle it with melted butter, sprinkle with browned breadcrumbs and cook in hot oven.

Five minutes before the end of cooking sprinkle with a small glass of *Trappistine* on each half lobster before singeing it with ½ *Trappistine* and ½ *Brandy*, and light it by pouring over it and basting it all the time until the flame is extinguished. Serve with beurre au fenouil made as per recipe below.

Beurre au Fenouil

Put in a saucepan some crushed peppercorns (ground not too finely), star-aniseed and fennel, half a glass of dry white wine, a tablespoon of vinegar, and allow it to cook until it is reduced to the quantity of a coffee spoon.

When the liquid boils put in 3 ozs. of butter in small pieces, boil it once rapidly, then take it off the fire. Finish with two tablespoonfuls of Hollandaise sauce. Season with salt to taste and strain before serving.

POULET VALLÉE D'AUGE

For four persons: sautée chicken in butter; salt and pepper it and cook it in a medium oven for half an hour. Pour over

3 ozs. of *Calvados* and blaze. Add 4 ozs. cream, stirring it into the juices in the pan, rectify the seasoning and serve.

PERNOD KEBABS

For six persons: Dice $1\frac{1}{2}$ lb. of beef sirloin and brush with mixture of 3 ozs. oil and 2 tsp. *Pernod*, salt and pepper. Slice an onion and add to beef, together with some crushed fennel seeds. Leave to marinate for 1-2 hours. Place beef, with slice of lean bacon, diced, sliced fennel and small onions, on skewers. Baste kebabs with the marinade and grill till cooked. Serve with hot rice.

ORANGES MYSTERIEUSES

One orange per person. Peel and remove pith, leaving orange whole. Shave off the finest possible layer of skin, discarding any of the pithy part of peel. Cut peel into matchstick pieces. Make a thick syrup using about 10 tbsp. water to 10 tbsp. sugar. Put peel into syrup and boil until it becomes caramelized. Take off heat and add 5 tbsp. *Glen Mist*. Allow to cool and put in fridge—the colder the better. Pour sauce over peeled oranges and decorate, if liked. Serve with whipped cream, to which a dash of *Glen Mist* can be added.

FROZEN MARSHMALLOW CAKE

For six persons: 3 ozs. digestive biscuits, 1 tbsp. drinking chocolate, 2 ozs. butter, 4 fl. ozs. milk, $\frac{1}{4}$ pt. double cream, 3 ozs. marshmallows, 2 fl. ozs. *Royal Mint-Chocolate Liqueur*. Melt the butter and stir in the finely crumbled biscuits and drinking chocolate. Press into foil lined cake tin, preferably spring form. Warm the milk with the marshmallows, stirring until they are dissolved. Whip the cream until stiff. Fold into milk/marshmallow mixture. Add liqueur. Pour into prepared case. Cover with foil and put into freezer for a minimum of 6 hours. Serve from freezer—do not defrost.

MARYLAND MINT

For dessert for four persons or cake for six: Using one

packet of chocolate chip cookies, half-pint whipped cream, miniature of *Royal Mint-Chocolate liqueur*. Dip each side of cookie in the liqueur. Spread a layer of cream on cookie and repeat process, laying treated cookies on a plate, lengthways, sticking each cookie along the plate to form a roll. Pipe additional cream along the top, sides and ends of the cake. Refrigerate and serve cold.

GLEN MIST SYLLABUB

For four persons: Half a pint of double cream, liqueur glass of *Glen Mist*, 1 tbsp. sugar, juice of a lemon and little grated rind. Mix altogether until stiff; pour into serving glasses and chill.

ALMOND CREAM

For 10 persons: Line a spring form pan with boudoir biscuits, cut in half (a dab of butter on the outside helps them to stick to the pan). Cream $\frac{1}{4}$ lb. of unsalted butter until soft, then add $\frac{1}{4}$ lb. castor sugar, creaming until light. Beat in $\frac{1}{4}$ lb. almonds, blanched and grated, together with 2 ozs. *Kirsch*. Fold this mixture into $\frac{3}{4}$ pint of whipped cream and put it into the pan. Chill and serve, decorated with more cream or fruit.

ROYAL MINT MOUSSE

For six persons: Line a spring form pan with boudoir biscuits (as above). Separate 6 eggs and beat yolks till creamy coloured. Dissolve $\frac{1}{2}$ oz. gelatine in little hot water. Beat whites until stiff, folding in 8 ozs. castor sugar. Combine all mixtures together, gently, adding 4 ozs. *Royal Mint-Chocolate liqueur*. Pour into prepared pan and leave to set. Decorate with chocolate flakes.

SOUFFLÉ AU GRAND MARNIER

For four persons: Pre-heat oven to 375°. Melt 3 tbsp. butter and stir in 3 tbsp. flour. Add 6 ozs. milk stirring with a wire whisk, and cook over low heat until mixture thickens. Stir in 4 egg yolks, lightly beaten; add grated orange rind and liqueur glass of *Grand Marnier*. Beat 6 egg whites until stiff and fold into soufflé mixture. Butter and sprinkle with sugar a soufflé dish, pour in mixture and bake 30 to 45 minutes.

COFFEE SPECIALITIES

Black coffee usually served with liqueur and cream (sugar if required).

Name of Speciality	*Liqueur or Spirit used*
Alpine Coffee	*Enzian liqueur or spirit*
Belgian Coffee	*Elixir d'Anvers*
Calypso Coffee	*Tia Maria*
Caribbean Coffee	*Rum*
Coffee of the Glens	*Glen Mist*
Dutch Coffee	*Genever*
French (or Royal) Coffee	*Cognac*
Gaelic Coffee	*Irish Whiskey*
German Coffee	*Kirsch*
Italian (or Witches') Coffee	*Strega*
Mexican Coffee	*Kahlúa*
Monks' Coffee	*Bénédictine; Chartreuse; Trappistine*
Normandy Coffee	*Calvados*
Prince Charles Coffee	*Drambuie*
Royal Mint Coffee	*Royal Mint-Chocolate*
Russian Coffee	*Vodka*
Scandinavian Coffee	*Aquavit*
Scotch Coffee	*Scotch Whisky*
Westphalian Coffee	*Steinhäger*

Chapter 25

BITTERS

A S their name suggests, these important additives to mixed
drinks have a bitter tang, and used to be known as
' Elixirs '—the Arab for Philosopher's Stone. The elixir of
alchemy was the wonder mixture that would transform base
metal into gold and prolong life indefinitely. The old saying
has it that " out of bitter comes sweetness." Good as they are
to stimulate the taste buds before a meal, bitters also have
their uses as a ' morning after ' corrective both for excesses
of food and drink.

Records have been preserved of ancient recipes for
medicines which are similar to some of the world-famous
bitters still in use.

Bitters are produced in two very distinct and separate
styles: Flavouring Bitters and Aromatic Bitters.

FLAVOURING BITTERS

Orange, peach, apricot bitters which add fruit flavour
and bouquet to mixed drinks and cocktails.

The best known flavouring bitters are the Pommeranzen
bitters (Elixir Longae Vitae) of German and Dutch producers,
Laws Peach bitters (English) and orange bitters from many
countries.

AROMATIC BITTERS

Are usually very distinctive, rich in bouquet and slightly pungent, designed to whet the appetite and stimulate the release of saliva juices in the mouth and gastric juices in the stomach. Most frequently used as additives to dry spirits—
Gin, Genever, Aquavit.

The best known aromatic bitters are:—

Campari (Italy)
Underberg (Germany)
Fernet-Branca (Italy)
Angostura (Trinidad)
Boonekamp (Holland)
Abbott's (U.S.A.)
Mampe Bitter Drops (Germany)

Amer Picon (France)
Unicum (Hungarian formula made in Italy)
Welling (Holland)
Secretat (France)
Toni-Kola (France)
Peychaud (U.S.A.)

These can be served as apéritifs (with ice and soda), or as digestives 'neat.'

Chapter 26

MIXED DRINKS AND COCKTAILS

MIXING liqueurs and spirits to prepare cocktails is very similar to a compounder preparing a new liqueur, who endeavours to produce an end product far more useful and enjoyable than any of his starting materials. Often a cocktail can be enjoyed by a person who dislikes the actual basic materials. The secret of the good cocktail is to present a new flavour and taste sensation, frequently with a fascinating texture and colour.

Many thousands of recipes are known and every year bartenders throughout the world concoct new mixtures, to celebrate a certain event, for a competition or even to try and please a particularly fastidious customer. Many of these cocktails are used only by their inventors, some are used nationally and very few reach the rank of international fame and general use.

The short selection is one of internationally renowned recipes and several newer ones of my own selection. Any bar displaying the flag of the U.K.B.G. (United Kingdom Bartenders Guild) will have a bartender in attendance well versed in the arts of mixing drinks, who will probably, on request, produce one of his own specialities or prepare a drink to meet your own particular taste preference.

119

* Available as ready mixed cocktails from various manufacturers. The ready-mixed cocktails are very popular in U.S.A.

Alaska
¾ Dry Gin
¼ Yellow Chartreuse
Shake and serve.

Alexander
⅓ Crème de Cacao
⅓ Fresh Cream
⅓ Brandy
Shake and serve.

Americano
1 oz. Campari
2 oz. sweet Vermouth
Ice, soda
Serve with twist of lemon peel.

Black Russian
½ Kahlúa
½ Vodka
Serve on the rocks.

Bloodiest Mary
⅓ Nicholoff Red Vodka
⅔ Tomato juice
2 dashes Angostura
Juice of ½ lemon

Bloody Mary
⅓ Vodka
⅔ Tomato juice
2 dashes Angostura
Juice of ½ lemon

Blue Moon
¾ Gin
¼ Crème Yvette
Mix and serve. .

Bronx
½ Gin ⅙ Vermouth (dry)
⅙ sweet Vermouth
⅙ Fresh orange juice
Shake and serve

Bullshot
1 tin condensed consommé
2 oz. Vodka or Gin
tsp. Worcester sauce
Juice of ½ lemon
Dash red pepper
Mix with ice and serve.

★Collins
Juice of ½ lemon
1 oz. Gin
tsp. sugar
Dash of Angostura
Cracked ice, soda
(John Collins—dry Gin
Tom Collins—Old Tom Gin)
Brandy, rum or whisky can replace gin.

Concord
½ Fresh Orange
¼ Calvados Un Trou Normand
¼ Grand Marnier
Stir, top up with Champagne or Sekt. Garnish with piece of pineapple on stick.

★Daiquiri (or Bacardi)
¾ Daiquiri rum (or Bacardi)
¼ Fresh lime or lemon juice
3 Dashes gomme, syrup or grenadine
Shake and serve.

Deauville
¼ Calvados Un Trou Normand
¼ Brandy
¼ Cointreau
¼ Fresh lemon juice

Gimlet
⅔ Dry gin
⅓ Rose's lime juice

Glen Mist
½ Glen Mist Scotch Whisky Liqueur
½ Scotch Whisky
Serve on the rocks.

Glen Mister
½ Glen Mist Scotch Whisky Liqueur
½ Rose's lime juice
Squeeze of lemon
Serve on the rocks.
(Tonic can be added for a long
    drink.)

Golden Dawn
¼ Calvados Un Trou Normand
¼ London Gin
¼ Apricot brandy
¼ Orange juice
Dash Grenadine

Hallmint
½ Royal Mint-Chocolate Liqueur
½ Cognac
2 Dashes Cointreau
Stir until cold and serve.

Harvard Cooler
2 ozs. Applejack (Calvados)
2 ozs. Lemon or lime juice
1 tsp. Powdered sugar
Ice and soda

Highball
Whisky, whiskey, gin, rum, brandy
1½ ozs. spirit, ice, dry ginger ale to
    taste
Squeeze of lemon rind.

Maid of Erin
⅓ Royal Mint Chocolate Liqueur
⅓ Fresh cream
⅓ Brandy
Shake and serve.

Manhattan
⅔ Rye Whiskey
⅓ Sweet Vermouth
Dash Angostura
Stir, strain and serve.

Margarita
1 oz. Tequila
½ oz. Triple Sec Curaçao
1 oz. lemon or fresh lime juice
Moisten rim of glass with fruit rind
and spin in salt. To be sipped over
salted edge.

Martini
⅔ Dry Gin
⅓ Dry Vermouth
Dash of orange bitters and twist of
lemon peel. For drier versions,
increase proportion of gin.

Mint Julep
4-6 sprigs fresh mint
½ tbsp. fine sugar
Minimum water. Crush mint in
the sugar solution. Add crushed
ice, slowly fill tumbler with 2 oz.
bourbon, decorate with mint, serve
with straw.

Mint-Royal
½ Royal Mint-Chocolate Liqueur
¼ Cognac
¼ Fresh lemon juice
Dash of egg white
Shake, serve cold

Monkey Gland
⅓ Pernod
⅓ Gin
⅓ Orange juice
Shake and serve.

Moscow Mule
2 oz. Vodka
1 oz. Lime juice
Ice and ginger beer
Decorate with mint.

Old Fashioned
Dash Angostura on sugar
Dissolve in minimum water
2 oz. Rye or Bourbon
Ice, ½ slice Orange

Piccadilly
⅔ London Gin
⅓ Dry Vermouth
Dash Grenadine
Dash Pernod

Pimm's
Various spirit cups, Nos. 1 to 6
Add fizzy lemonade to taste; garnish with orange, lemon, cucumber, add ice. A sprig of borage is the ultimate refinement.
Serve with straws.

Pink Lady
½ White of Egg
2 ozs. Gin
1 tsp. Grenadine
Shake and serve

Planter's Punch
1 Dash Angostura
1 oz. lime or lemon juice
1 tsp. Grenadine
2 ozs. Rum
Soda, ice
Serve with small slices of citrus fruit.

Pousse Café
Mixed drinks of expertly layered liqueurs of different colours. Differences of density prevent mixing of the ingredients which must be poured slowly, preferably over the back of a spoon.

There are several recipes available. Pour the liqueurs in sequence slowly over the back of a teaspoon:

⅙ Grenadine
⅙ Maraschino
⅙ Green Crème de Menthe
⅙ Crème de Violettes
⅙ Chartreuse
⅙ Brandy
(Esquire drink book)

⅐ Sloe Gin
⅐ Curaçao, triple sec
⅐ Apricot Brandy
⅐ Curaçao
⅐ Liqueur d'Or
⅐ Crème de Menthe
⅐ Crème de Cacao
(Bols recipe)

Q4
¼ Royal Mint-Chocolate Liqueur
¼ Chartreuse
¼ Cinzano Bianco
¼ Scotch Whisky

Rob Roy
½ Scotch Whisky
½ Sweet Vermouth
Dash Angostura
1 Cherry
Stir and serve.

Royal Mint-Ball
$^1/_5$ Royal Mint-Chocolate Liqueur
$^1/_5$ Advocaat
$^3/_5$ (approx.) sparkling lemonade to taste
Serve cold.

Rusty Nail
⅔ Scotch Whisky
⅓ Drambuie
Twist of lemon
Serve on the rocks.

Scotch Mist
2 ozs. Scotch Whisky
Cracked ice
Twist of lemon peel

Screwdriver
½ Vodka
½ Orange juice
Ice

Sidecar
½ Brandy
¼ Cointreau
¼ Lemon juice
Shake and serve.

Snowball
Advocaat
Dash of lime
Sparkling lemonade to taste

*Sour
Brandy, Gin, Rum, Whisky*
1 oz. Lemon juice
½ tsp. Sugar
2 ozs. selected spirit
Shake, add soda and slice of lemon

Stinger
⅔ Brandy
⅓ Crème de Menthe
Mix and serve.

Whisky Mac
½ Scotch Whisky
½ Ginger Wine

White Lady
½ Gin
¼ Cointreau
¼ Lemon juice
Shake and serve

*Vodkatini
⅔ Vodka
⅓ Dry Vermouth
Dash of orange bitters
Twist of lemon peel
For drier versions increase proportion of Vodka

APPENDIX

COUNCIL OF EUROPE DEFINITION OF LIQUEURS
PROVISIONAL DEFINITIONS

ARTICLE 5—Definition of liqueurs and liqueur spirits:

1. ' Liqueurs ' and more generally, ' Liqueur Spirits ' mean spirits of which the essential characteristic is the presence of sugars and aromatising substances, naturally present or added.

2. Liqueurs proper must contain at least 100 g. of sugar per litre (expressed as sucrose).

3. Liqueurs known as ' cream liqueurs ' must contain at least 400 g. of sugars per litre (expressed as sucrose).

4. Dry liqueurs and like beverages (bitters, anisettes, etc.), must not contain more than 100 g. of sugars per litre (expressed as sucrose).

ARTICLE 5 bis—Definition of aromatising substances:

Aromatising substances, usually of vegetable or animal origin, which must not be harmful to health in the doses found in finished products, mean:

(a) *Natural aromatising or flavouring substances* which are aromatising substances of vegetable or animal origin, existing in nature and used either fresh or after conservation by a physical process or after having undergone appropriate treatment such as: drying, heating, roasting, fermentation, enzymatic treatment.

(b) *Natural flavourings* which are complex aromatising substances (essential oils, infusions, extracts, alcolates, etc.), obtained from natural substances by physical processes such as extraction, pressing, distillation.

(c) *The components of flavouring* which are aromatising substances having a defined chemical constitution and are present in natural flavourings; these components are obtained from natural aromatic substances by means of a physical separation treatment or a physiochemical or chemical separation treatment.

(d) *The components of synthetic flavourings* which are aromatising substances whose chemical composition is identical to that of substances existing in nature.

(e) *Artificial aromatic substances* which have no known natural source and are prepared by synthetic industrial process.

' Sugars ' are defined as follows:

All sweetening substances composed of soluble carbohydrates such as, for example, sucrose, glucose, fructose, invert sugar, maltose, lactose.

(N.B.—' Sugar ' in the singular always means sucrose.)

BIBLIOGRAPHY

Booth's Handbook of Cocktails and Mixed Drinks (*Doxat*, London 1966).
Die Frucht Liköre (*Hartman*, Berlin 1952).
Drogen in der Spirituosen Industrie (*Hartman*, Berlin 1952).
Esquire Drink Book (*Birmingham*, London 1957).
Grossman's Guide to Wines, Spirits and Beers (New York 1964).
Guide to Drinks (U.K.B.G., London 1965)
Liqueurs (*M. I. Fischer*, London 1951).

Publications of the following Associations:
    Liqueur Importers Association.
    Scotch Whisky Association.
    Wine and Spirit Association of Great Britain.

Publications of the following Trade Journals:
    BAR, Ontario.
    BEVERAGE MEDIA, U.S.A.
    HARPERS WINE AND SPIRIT GAZETTE, London.
    RIDLEY'S, London.
    WINE AND SPIRIT TRADE RECORD, London.
    WINE AND SPIRIT TRADE REVIEW, London.
Rezeptbuch fur Diestillateure (*Meiniger*, Neustadt 1952).
Spirituosen Jahrbuch 1967 (*Versuchs und Lehranstalt*, Berlin).
Traite de la Fabrication des Liqueurs (*Duplais*, Paris 1866).
Trinkbranntweine und Liköre (*Wustenfeld*, Berlin 1953).
The Whiskies of Scotland (*McDowell*, London 1967).
Various Articles and Notes by the late W. H. Nithsdale, O.B.E. (London 1958, *et seq*).
Wines and Spirits (*Massee*, New York 1961).

ACKNOWLEDGEMENT FOR PHOTOGRAPHS

Colour Jacket and End-Plates—Percy Hennell.

Plates 1, 3, 4, 6—Cusenier, Paris.

Plates 2, 10—Société de la Bénédictine, Fécamp.

Plate 5—Vve. Champion, Bordeaux.

Plate 7—The Glen Mist Liqueur Company, London.

Plate 8—Jas. Hennessy & Co., Cognac.

Plate 9—Erven Lucas Bols, Schiedam.

Plate 11—Mampe, Berlin.

Plates 12, 13—Scotch Whisky Association, London.

Plate 14—James Burrough Ltd., London.

———

Whisky Distillery Diagram, reproduced by permission of Professor R. J. S. McDowall (The Whiskies of Scotland—*John Murray*, London).

" Liqueurograph," reproduced by permission of Wineographs, London

" Coffee Specialities "—Berni Inns, Schooner Inns, *et al.*

· INDEX

127

INDEX